PERSONS OF INTEREST.
THE OUTSIDERS

PERSONS OF INTEREST.
THE OUTSIDERS

25 lessons learnt from 11 interviews with people living life differently

GLENNYS MARSDON

Zeitgeist Creations

"This is great stuff, I feel honoured and in good company. I am intrigued and eager to read on." Tineke Van der Eecken

"I'm so chuffed to be profiled beside legends like iconic comedian Tim Ferguson and international cartoonist Jason Chatfield, among many other inspiring people. This is one of the most indepth interviews I've ever given, ranging from professional to very personal. I feel it would be great for people deciding whether or not to pursue their dreams or not (spoiler alert: YES DO IT, but the book can better tell you Why and How)." Holden Sheppard.

"Eleven ways of living, of being, of doing collected and presented by the person of most interest of all." Frances Maber.

For Don, Ailsa, Geoff
My protectors and mentors growing up.

Part proceeds go to medical research (Cancer
and MS)

CONTENTS

CHAPTER 1

INTRODUCTION

People have always interested me, especially those living outside the square, doing things differently. Given this, it was probably inevitable that I'd end up studying psychology.

For the past three decades my paid and volunteer work has enabled me to meet a vast array of fascinating people. I've often wondered why their names haven't appeared amongst the models and sportsmen regularly featured in Top 100 People articles. For whatever reason these often-quiet achievers, don't receive the recognition they deserve.

As another year passed by without seeing their names, I thought there was only one thing to do, I'd shine a light on them myself. At the very least it would enable them to hear about each other and who knows where that might end?

Having spent over 15 years researching the Year 11/12 school segment, I also thought the students might be interested hearing about people living outside the norm. To learn that there is more than one way to live an interesting, meaningful life. One that goes beyond the normal pathways. Similarly, I hoped the stories might catch the attention of a few School Psychologists or Career Counsellors.

Who to interview?

The first task was to narrow down who, amongst the plethora of interesting people I've been lucky enough to meet, should be interviewed. To help with this I set the following criteria.

The person had to be:

Living an interesting life that was somewhat outside the norm;

What they were doing would be meaningful or of interest to others;

Their story had not been heavily featured in the media i.e. they were not yet a household name, yet.

And so I set about identifying 10 people to interview.

Interviewees were recruited through the Snowballing Technique, that is people were asked if they knew anyone living an interesting life. Those identified were sent a self-completion questionnaire and in some cases a follow up interview was conducted.

The search stretched over three years, thanks in part to Covid19 halting everything for one of those years.

To date we have stories from 11 *Persons of Interest* across a broad range of genders, age groups, physical ability, sexuality ethnicity and industries including an:

- International Cartoonist/Stand-up Comedian;
- Criminologist/Domestic Violence Mediator turned jewellery designer:
- General Practitioner who flies herself to rural appointments;
- OBE wielding, octogenarian Wildlife Educator, who was also the first female State Director of a Commonwealth Public Service Department;
- The fastest Australian with MS on a motorbike;
- Female Film Director/Developer.

I will admit that some of these people have received an amount of media attention, but they are not household names. There were two exceptions to the rule that simply could not be overlook.

First up comedy legend, film director, writer and teacher Tim Ferguson of *Doug Anthony All Stars* fame. Along the way I was given the opportunity to interview this fascinating man. While definitely not meeting the "under the radar" criteria, who could pass up such an opportunity.

Secondly the book contains a case study of Ian Usher, best known as *"The Man Who Sold His Life On eBay"*. Usher turned a difficult period of his life to his advantage and has spent the last 13 years living a life that is the epitome of interesting and outside the norm. In doing so he has received some international recognition. I'm sure that after reading his story you will agree his story had to be included.

Twenty Five Lessons Learnt

As is often the case when you start interviewing a random group of people, unexpected patterns emerge.

While I knew the interviewees' current lives did not fit the norm, I was surprised to hear several say they didn't fit in at school or society when growing up. These admissions got me thinking about the idea of Outsiders. What is the current perception on an Outsider? Is there a segment of "Hidden Outsiders"? This is one of the **Twenty Five Lessons Learnt** that we discuss in the final chapter. Having spent over three decades interviewing people and distilling the millions of hours of conversation into key learnings, my researcher brain could not write *The End* without siphoning out some lessons learnt. I hope you find them interesting.

Do you know anyone?

This is by no means the end to this project. The beauty of an eBook is I can update the volume whenever a new story comes to light. If you know someone who should be featured please let me know. In the meantime, I hope you find these stories as interesting and motivating as I did.

Thank you

To the people profiled in this book, many thanks for your time, honesty and most importantly patience. It was an absolute pleasure meeting every one of you. I wish you well on your next endeavour as I know you won't be sitting still.

Glennys

CHAPTER 2

TIM FERGUSON
(Comedy icon/Director/ Author)

Tim Ferguson
Credit: Jeremy Belinfonte

PROFILE

Tim Ferguson is a much-loved Australian comedian, film director, screenwriter, author and teacher.

Ferguson first came to prominence as a member of the musical comedy trio *Doug Anthony All Stars*. Having taken the Edinburgh Festival Fringe by storm in 1987. The group went on to appear on UK Channel 4 television show *Friday Night Live*. The *All Stars* also appeared on *The Big Gig* and their own *DAAS Kapital*.

After the group disbanded in 1994 Ferguson went on to develop a plethora of writing, television and film projects including: hosting game show *Don't Forget Your Toothbrush;* co-writing and hosting eight series and twelve one-hour specials of his comedy clip show *Unreal TV* and co-producer of the sitcom *Shock Jock*.

His film writing credits include: *Spin Out* and *The BBQ*. He also starred in *That's Not My Dog* and appeared in *Fat Pizza*.

Ferguson has also penned a novel, *Left, Right and Centre: A Tale of Greed, Sex and Power* and has written various opinion pieces and articles for *The Age, The Sydney Morning Herald and The Times*.

In 2013, after a life with MS he wrote his autobiography *Carry a Big Stick: A Life of Laughter, Friendship and MS*, which he also toured.

From 2016 he has taught various comedy writing courses, and his book *The Cheeky Monkey - Writing Narrative Comedy* is seen as a definitive manual for writers.

Instagram @therealtimferguson
www.cheekymonkey.com

INTERVIEW

Apart from family, what were your greatest one or two achievements?

The path less trodden.

Showing people that even disability can open up doors. When one door closes you have to kick in another one. It's a lesson that's worked before I had MS and will continue. Looking for the path and trying to stay ahead of the changes.

Being positive. If your boat sinks in the ocean, people who stay positive survive.

Anything missed out on by living this life?

No, nothing I wanted to do.

Because everything is always changing you've always got the chance and the time to change tracks. If I did want to become a lawyer I could do that. It'd take less time, it's only three years. There's a reason you can be a law student, get drunk, screw everybody and still come out with honors. What's university for ... like learning ... really? The assumption is you learn enough, and then you'll learn more on the job.

How often have you thought about giving up?

Never.

It's weird. I had people tell me "why don't you just go work at Safeway, it'll be a lot less risk and you'll become a manager in five years." I don't think I'd ever fit into that kind of pattern. It's not bloody-mindedness ... I don't think I'm built to surrender. I don't think I'd fit into someone else's system.

It goes way back to going to nine schools. I was a good kid I didn't get kicked out. My parents moved. This constant change developed some great independence in my brothers and I. Fierce independence means I am happy to back myself. I know these are my strengths, this is what I've spent years practicing. There's no point putting it aside because it's difficult.

Now doing stand-up comedy sitting down I just have to work out a way to do it. I do a lot of physiotherapy, I listen to what my body is telling me and treat it well. You're allowed to drink, smoke pot, get into fist fights ... but I try to keep that down to one giant bout every week.

What have you learnt from any difficulties or failures along the way?

Keep going, keep developing your skills.

If there's a lot of competition, then look at your market and find the gap.

What motivates or drives you?

Control.

Being a freelance writer, you could work for the West Australian and get paid $500 for a small piece or $1000 for a larger piece, but then you wouldn't be the boss ... and you'd have to deal with them.

Quite often a rejection is not personal. If you write something and an editor says, "we're not doing that at the moment, it's nothing personal we've just done something big on doctors, or we just did that". People do that with movies and TV too. So, you go away and you come up with something else. It does leave you in control, because you're the one who wakes up the day after and says I will invent a new project. If you're even a little creative, you'll have a list of *Crap I Want To Do.*

Like any creative enterprise, creativity stops at the beginning. Say I say that I will do a thing about racehorses, and from then on it's about craft. It's the skill, it's writing it again and again. You don't really get a lot of inspiration. You can feel inspired that it's working, but the rest of the time comedy, like writing, you just have to do it again and again and again.

There is no difference to dentistry, being an astronaut and being a comedian, they all take practice. The first time you try it ... like going to space, you will die. You just have to keep practicing.

Comedy relies not so much on instinct as in being comfortable in what you are doing. Like writing a book, you'll be comfortable that you know enough stuff, now the question is how to structure it. How to finish each section with an "oh", a "hmm" and then how to open the next section with something amusing, frightening, unnerving, confronting, or confusing so people have to read more.

No one is a natural comedian. You can have people who are funny at school or in life, they usually make terrible comedians because the skills don't transfer. The audience doesn't know them. To make people laugh you have to surprise them with something that figures ... that's it.

If you look at the great comics like Robyn Williams, he was naturally a risk taker. He was very funny and could improvise wonderful stuff. Maybe he was good at that in high school, but he had to do it again and again.

My favourites are all the Americans ... Steve Martin, Martin Short, Chevy Chase. They just had to do it again and again.

Why go back on the road?

I started working with Marc Gracie, our tour promoter from the *All Stars*. I'd also done a lot of short term one offs for corporate, and found audiences laugh. I wrote a book *Carry A Big Stick* and it was Gracie's idea that it could be a show.

It was about having good people around.

What else helped you get to where you are?

Practice, practice. Comedy is no different to anything else.

A lot of people want to try stand-up comedy now. Some want to do it as therapy so they can say "I did that, I always wanted to do it, I was terrified, I did it and that will be it". Good on them. But they're getting in our way … in the way of other people who really want to be comedians.

There were no people in the 1980's who wanted to be a comedian, we met nobody. The only comedians we met were a bit embarrassed about it. Even actors would say to us "oh that's a shame, can't you act?" It wasn't seen as a career path back then. We didn't tell them but we knew … and the comedians we worked with knew … that comedy was the fastest way to have a more solid career. Because you are in charge of it. You're not waiting for a director to pick you out of ten people who were just as good.

Personality.

There's an element of being a bit of a sociopath, where part of you is unable to take no for an answer. It's not being strong, forceful or brave, it's just there's a part in their makeup that is unable to hear the word 'no'. The assumption is if someone does say no, then they must be mad. Even if we know they've got a point, and we discover that later, they're still mad.

My brother had a great approach, he was in sales for a magazine. He said with clients who wouldn't buy ad space he'd say "okay but the door is always open". What they didn't understand was that this meant their door was always open to him, the reverse ... he would always come back. When people called the magazine editors to complain, my brother would call them back to apologise and then go on to explain "it was only because we had such amazing deals at the moment".

You have to have something in your mind that can ignore your doubts. If you don't have that, don't worry you can develop it. Just ignore your doubts. While everybody is following their doubts, you can be the bubble that rises. Better to find out later that you were wrong, than assume you are going to be wrong.

What main message(s) or advice would you give others?

You don't have to go to university or TAFE or any other damn place. If you've got an idea of what you want to do, and you have some plan about how you can do it, and how you can learn more about it, do it.

Look at Richard Branson, Harvey and Norman. Branson and Harvey are dyslexic. It's a big thing with billionaires. It's because everybody else's standards don't apply.

If it feels right give it a shot. Particularly if you are young, you might as well burn the candle. And if we're talking to school kids in this book ... it's driving your parents nuts and that's got to be good.

Has planning or goal setting been part of your process?

It's been and continues to be a completely organic experience. It's not that I don't have a plan, it's just plans keep finishing.

You want to do something say you want to make a movie ... eventually you make that movie and that ends so you start the slow process of making another one. Or doing this tour and then when we've done everywhere, now we have to come up with a new angle.

It started with *All Stars* and it was a case of see which doors open when you kick them and go through it. Kick them as hard as you can and keep your fingers crossed.

Some people would say there's too much risk involved, the chances of going broke or getting fired are far too great ... and in a way they are. But if you practice what you do, and you get good at what you do, you can usually find somewhere to do it, and new people to do it with.

So, if you do a show and it's just not funny and nobody gets it and you fall flat on your face and it ends up in the papers that you are not funny, you can't stop. You can try to come up with something that is funny. So, you fall back on your skills and hope they work.

Growing up, to what extent did you feel different from your peers?

Oh yeah. I was outside. Because I was always the new kid at every school until just before I would have to leave. That fed a kind of opportunism. There is an opportunism to being outside things. It means the conventions and rules don't really apply.

It means when someone is talking about careers you don't immediately think about the standard stuff ... which is important stuff we all need doctors ... but the fact that it's the convention doesn't touch the sides.

When people were talking about careers, I started a theatre company with my mates when I was 19. It was called *Black Inc* and we did a whole bunch of plays. That's how we survived, while everybody else was at university.

I sound like I went to university, but I didn't. It's because of my Singapore accent. It sounds like I went there, so why would I bother.

If the Police listed you as a person of interest what would it be for?

Troublemaking in places where you normally wouldn't expect trouble. Like on national television in prime time.

Doing things that are borderline illegal, one with dynamite for example.

What is the current project you are working on?

Note: The tour Tim talked about at that time have since finished. To keep up to date with his tours check out his website and Instagram.

Also watch out for Tim's comedy writing courses, and his book *The Cheeky Monkey - Writing Narrative Comedy*. I can attest to them both being brilliant for any emerging writer. His most recent course is a *Sitcom Screenwriting Comedy Class*.

CHAPTER 3

Dr OLGA WARD
(General Practitioner Pink Plane Pilot)

Dr Olga Ward
Credit: Dr Olga Ward

PROFILE

Olga Ward has been a procedural rural General Practitioner since 1994. She was also one of the first GPs in Australia to obtain a FARGP in surgery as well as in adult internal medicine.

She maintains active involvement with country work and since 2015 has worked with the Rural Health Outreach Foundation. Her work services the areas of Bruce Rock, Westonia, Narembeen, Merredin and Narrogin Hospitals.

In addition, she has conducted regular clinics with the Royal Flying Doctors Service, which sees her flying herself to remote patients.

Ward also enjoys teaching students and working in palliative care and aviation medicine. Apart from general practice, her other work involves the support and education of rural GPs.

Over the past 16 years she has intermittently presented courses at CTEC, UWA on topics including Emergency Procedures and the Cutting Edge series. She has been on the editorial advisory committee for Medial Forum WA Magazine for over ten years.

In 2017 she received the Rural Health West/Wesfarmers award for remote and clinically challenging medicine.

In terms of social media she can be found on LinkedIn using Dr Olga Ward.

INTERVIEW

Apart from family, what were your greatest one or two achievements?

Making General Practice my own job. Being able to do it with my own style, so it was reflecting both my interests as well as the needs of my community.

Staying in the WASO Chorus, I meltdown in auditions.

How is the life you've lived different from others?

I'm a pilot and a doctor.

This means I would like things to be as boring as possible. Take off, get there fast, land, sit on a veranda with and gin and tonic, and see patients who don't have unicorn-rarity symptoms. This doesn't happen, but one can yearn for the quiet life.

I love to do, see and experience loads of different things. This gives me a very broad range.

I prefer to fly my plane to work in the bush, weather permitting. When I bought my plane, it was white with a burgundy and gold stripe. But it had been in the red dirt for so long that when it went to Jandakot for maintenance, and was parked on the grass next to blue and white planes, I got loads of stick about how my plane was actually pink. The moniker "pink plane" stuck. When I had a repaint, I chose a brand new official Piper aircraft colour called "Piper Magenta". The plane now has dark pink on the belly and wingtips. I like it a lot.

I prefer to ride a motorcycle round Perth, again weather permitting, and the home visit bag doesn't fit well onto the bike.

I spend a lot of time exercising my rescue kelpie, I love to sing and am learning to play the oboe. I do not highly recommend 50 years of age as a starting age for such a difficult instrument, but it will sound lovely one day.

How did you come to live this type of life?

This is a very long story. I went into rural practice because my husband was training to be an Anglican priest and they are usually posted rural for the first 5 to10 years. I did the training for rural practice and found it to be the best fit for an enquiring mind that I could have possibly found.

My husband changed careers, but I'd done the training by then and loved it. I always wanted to fly so I used rural practice work to give me a reason to fly and keep flying as part of my work.

When I left full time rural practice I was as burnt out as one can possibly be. But the passion for rural generalism never left me. Pretty much as soon as we moved back to Perth, I went straight back to part time FIFO rural practice and support for other rural GPs.

What was your biggest challenge in achieving your goals or getting to where you are now?

Bureaucracy seems to be a big challenge for me.

I don't fit neatly into anyone's tick chart. They usually respond to this with obstruction rather than talking about how we can use my, or any skills, to advantage.

How often have you thought about giving up?

I thought about giving up a few times.

This was due to time, sleep and challenging cases that are emotionally, as well as medically, challenging.

Also trying to deal with bureaucrats who just want to implement lists and protocols rather than actually look at the issues at hand.

Exhaustion, physical and mental, is very real. There is no quarter in the system, or from the patients for a sub- par doctor.

What have you learnt from any difficulties or failures along the way?

Squeaky wheels get oiled. Joining committees and making changes from the inside is frustratingly slow, but change can be made. It might just be too late for the change to benefit me.

Singing can be improved with practice, as can oboe playing.

Physiotherapy exercises are most effective when they are actually done.

What motivates or drives you?

It's about the patients. The community. The desire to give back.

For the singing and oboe it's about the music.

What else helped you get to where you are?

I'm quite tenacious.

I believe in doing a good job, not just an adequate job.

I plan a lot, out of necessity, but I'm flexible enough to make changes.

I was diagnosed with cancer five years ago and since then I'm even more keen to grasp any opportunities that come past. I'm pleased to say I just got the all clear.

Has planning or goal setting been part of your process?

I'm fairly goal focussed. But I've had to let a few go due to illness or exhaustion or family crises.

What main message(s) or advice would you give others?

Have a red hot go. Talk to your mates. Love something outside of work. Get a dog.

Growing up, to what extent did you feel different from your peers?

A lot.

I'm the child of a Palestinian refugee and a mystery dad who might have been from outback Queensland, or as my birth certificate states from Sheffield UK.

I was an only child, darker skinned, obsessed with reading, not good at sport, overweight, a good deal younger than my school cohort and with parents old enough to be grandparents or older. My mother was 44 years old when I was born, and Dad was pushing 60. We didn't do the same stuff that my peers did after school or on holidays. I was used to being alone.

I liked classical music, dance, reading, languages and dog walking. The norm at my school was pop or rock, tennis, camping and swimming training.

If the police listed you as a person of interest what would it be for?

Oppositional. And a bit of a shit stirrer.

What is the current project you are working on?

I'm hoping for a Churchill Fellowship to have a look at the way other systems support rural generalists and proceduralists.

I'm working on playing the oboe well enough to join the WA Doctors' Orchestra at some stage.

CHAPTER 4

TINEKE VAN DER EECKEN (Mediator/ Internationally exhibited artist)

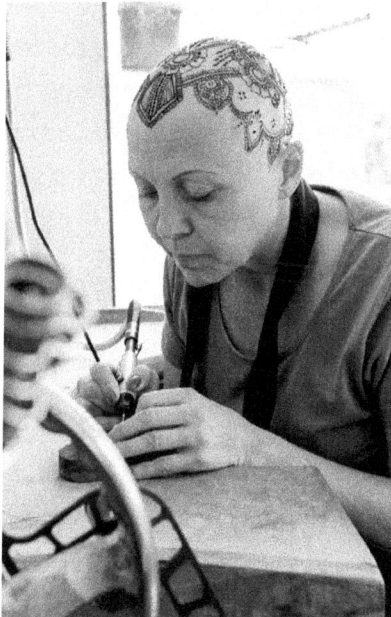

Tineke Van der Eecken
Credit: James Kerr

PROFILE

Tineke Van der Eecken is a writer and artist who works in conflict resolution. She is the author of *Cafe d'Afrique* (2012) and *Traverse* (published in 2018 after being shortlisted in the TAG Hungerford Award) and writer/ performer of multilingual poetry.

As a former board member of WritingWA, an alumna of Leadership Western Australia, co-founder of *Poetry d'Amour* and BRINK renewable Arts program, Tineke is known in (and continues to contribute to) the Perth arts sector. Less known is that she is a nationally accredited Mediator working in restorative justice and has been working in victim-offender mediation since 2014. These experiences have inspired her current writing project, a novel set in the West Australian justice system. When possible, she chooses the creative path.

Van der Eecken studied Jewellery Design and Fabrication at the West-Australian TAFE as a mature-aged student and quickly developed her own style. She combines working with wire with traditional jewellery–making techniques, the setting of stones and 'organic casting', to recreate original forms from nature in previous metal.

In 2002 she established *'Tineke Creations'* as a sustainable business. She has been designing and exhibiting work as a visual artist in jewellery and small sculptures since 2004 including exhibitions in Australia, Belgium and the United Kingdom for over 15 years.

This follows an international career in Gender Equality, Women in Development, Children in Development and small enterprise creation with the UN International Labour Office, Unicef, the Flemish Technical Aid etc. These positions were mainly based in Central and Southern Africa.

Born in Belgium she holds a Degree in Criminological Sciences, has two grown-up children and resides in Fremantle, Western Australia.

She has lived and worked in many countries, including Burundi, Zambia and Australia and travelled to remote parts of the world such as Papua New Guinea, Easter Island and Madagascar.

www.tinekecreations.com

www.readtraverse.com

Facebook as TinekeVanderEeckenAuthor and Tineke Creations

Instagram @TinekeCreations

INTERVIEW

Apart from family, what were your greatest one or two achievements?

I had a high-flying initial career working for the United Nations and was geared towards working in politics in Belgium, which could be considered big achievements.

What I consider my biggest achievements is to have had the chance later in life (at age 35) to develop my creative skills, to reconnect with my earlier passion for language and literature, write poetry and books. Plus to have since developed a successful creative business designing and making jewellery, which connects me with nature, forms part of this achievement.

Secondly, I have been able to turn a weakness into a strength by becoming a Mediator and working in conflict resolution, which has changed my life. I used to avoid conflict because of experiences as a child. Now I work in prisons and with very vulnerable people (including victims) in the community, managing the most delicate communication processes successfully.

How do you think the life you've lived is different others?

I would say "lives' not life as I seem to be living many lives and they keep changing. I grew up in Belgium and ventured out as soon as I graduated as a Criminologist.

I travelled around Papua New Guinea on my own at the age of 22, and at 24 I had a contract with the United Nations to work with women in Burundi, and later in Zambia. I was involved in many worthwhile projects designed to improve education for vulnerable children and to fight women's poverty.

While working in Africa I fell in love with the vibrant African cultural scene and set up the first cultural restaurant in Lusaka.

Two years later I was back in Belgium being groomed for a political career and advising the Minister on new approaches in international co-operation with African countries.

When my then husband (a Belgian geologist I had met in Zambia) announced he was going to do his PHD studies in Australia, I reluctantly followed him with our two small children in tow, to Perth. I had to start from zero again.

Then in 2001, I decided to do what I had not had time for, to hone my creative writing skills and write a book. I also had some gemstones given to me as a farewell present when leaving Zambia, and wanted to create jewellery. So I enrolled in a TAFE course to make and design jewellery.

Since then, I have been an investigative journalist, a CEO of a medical research institute, a Board member for a number of not-for-profits, a marketing and PR manager, a writer, a jeweller, and a mediator in prisons.

I travel to Belgium on a regular basis to visit my family and friends but in the meantime, I call Fremantle home.

I missed Africa however and made my experiences the object of my first book, *Café d'Afrique* (published 2009).

There was another big change in direction in 2006 when my husband accepted a job in the United Kingdom and we moved to the Midlands in England.

While I tried hard to establish myself in that country as a jewellery designer-maker and a writer, my husband worked on a big project in Madagascar.

He fell in love with a colleague which caused the inevitable marriage crisis. But rather than giving up on our family I decided to help him work through it and accompanied him on his last expedition to Madagascar.

Officially it was to document his work trip … unofficially to find out if our family, if we as a couple, had a future. I knew I would have material for a book. As a result *Traverse* was published in late 2018.

How did you come to live this type of life?

I went with the flow.

I always followed the more interesting path, not what made money, but where I could make a difference.

Where I could discover something about myself and others, an experience that would make me grow as a person.

How often have you thought about giving up?

I tended to give up when a work or other situation became too tense or had too much conflict.

The writing of each of my two books has probably been the toughest and I asked myself numerous times why I would not simply give up and leave it. Who was waiting for these books anyway?

Each of the books have taken me 10 years to write and see published. I am now 2 years into my next book.

Knowing it takes time gives me comfort. It means I can write when I can make the time for it, and when I feel excited about doing it.

What was your biggest challenge in achieving your goals or getting to where you are now?

Life is a balancing act.

Moving country and trying to keep the family together forced me to make tough decisions and sacrifices. I saw these challenges ultimately as opportunities to make the best out of a difficult situation.

I trained in Mediation and Conflict Resolution, and honed skills I felt I had not developed sufficiently.

I learnt to speak my truth and develop deep listening skills. Divorcing my partner after 19 years was an outcome of facing and speaking the truth, and the start of a new direction in life. The decision gave me wings, but also made creative work more risky financially.

To live a creative life requires some stability and focus. To counter this, I have developed my skills and run an Airbnb business.

In May 2015 I was diagnosed with breast cancer. It was a small aggressive tumour I discovered by chance. I was 48 and it would likely not have shown on a mammogram if I had had one. It was in its first stage, which only lasts for 8-12 weeks, and had not spread. I had a lumpectomy, followed by 6 months of chemotherapy 2 months of radiotherapy, which decimated my health and even mental resilience.

It took me 2 years to regain enough focus and memory to read a novel on the page. But I managed to do a Leadership W.A. course which I had applied for previously. The timing was odd, and I felt very weak. What 'leader' is left in you when you're on the couch sleeping all day? I had to answer many questions about myself, and re-assess leadership skills and values in different contexts, while listening to and meeting other 'leaders' in business, government, and not-for-profits.

During that time I had an exhibition of jewellery I had made before, with portrait photography of myself as a maker by James Kerr, and poetry by writing friends in return for a piece of jewellery. Having poets and friends responding to my creative work helped me regain confidence in myself.

What have you learnt from any difficulties or failures along the way?

That nothing is a given.

You need to work hard to get what you want, but with dedication and passion anything becomes possible.

I know what my shortcomings are but being a positive I don't let that hold me from taking on a challenge.

Even though I do many different things I always aim to work at a high professional standard.

I see difficulties as opportunities to learn and to do better.

I keep learning and seldom get bored.

What motivates or drives you?

I don't believe in giving up. I want to prove to myself that I can achieve what I set out to do, even if it takes 10 or 20 years.

If I love what I am doing then I just keep at it. I should not be hung-up about anybody else's expectations. Things will work out if they are meant to be.

With my books, I really wanted to share those stories. To know is to love, and ultimately if we all shared our story the world would be a more understanding place.

What else helped you get to where you are?

I like being MOVED.

It means that what I make comes from the heart and it goes out to another's heart.

I believe the world is a better place than the media portray it to be. I am surrounded by people who care, and I care too. Sharing this makes you feel good about where we are, here and now.

Other people encourage me. They buy my jewellery and talk about it many years after. They hear my poetry or read my books and are moved by it.

Personality traits

I come from a family of strong women. My mother was a politician, my aunties are strong independent women who worked to help families facing domestic violence. It is ironic that in spite of their activism and strength there was domestic violence in our home. I grew up in fear of my father's violence and other harmful behaviour.

Overcoming domestic violence in my own life has given me a resilience and strategies to cope with hardship, while I recognise vulnerability because it is in me too. I can empathise.

I have learnt to recognise my scars and to forgive and to not be overwhelmed and ruled by my past experiences.

I feel very strongly that we are collectively responsible to make this world a better and safer place, in particular for women and for children.

Has planning or goal setting been part of your process?

For my jewellery I work six months to a year ahead if it's an exhibition, or even more. Often, I will have been collecting photos and materials resulting in an idea or concept for a show, or a new series of work.

For private orders of jewellery I usually ask plenty of time to create, which can be anything from 6 weeks to 6 months.

For my poetry it happens 'in the moment'. Often the poems don't see the light of day until I re-read them, edit and group them for a publication.

My books take much longer to prepare and write and publish. On average 10 years. The planning arises from the experience.

Cafe d'Afrique was based on events during the 1990s until 2000. I wrote it between 2002 and 2008 and edited it again until it was published in 2012. *Traverse* was published in 2018, the trip it is based on happened in 2007.

What main message(s) or advice would you give others?

Don't overthink where you are headed because life is more interesting if you allow things to emerge.

Be honest with yourself, follow your sixth sense.

Seek to work with people who align with your values and have skills that complement yours.

To what extent did you feel you fitted into society when you were growing up? (5 is felt on the outside, 1 easy fitted in).

Score 4 out of 5

I had the communication skills to get along with people from different walks of life, but I often felt judged because people 'knew' my famous mother and projected expectations on me that I felt unprepared for.

As a creative child I was interested in things that were not mainstream, and I was stubborn enough to refuse to follow what everyone else did. For instance, I did not like watching television and I did anything to avoid the obligatory school reading and literature list.

I had many friends but only few I felt a deep connection with.

I experimented with risky behaviour as a young teenager and had a strong sense that I wanted to discover life on my own terms.

If the police listed you as a person of interest what would it be for?

They may stumble on some stories of crimes and misdemeanours I was lucky, or let's say privileged enough, to get away with it.

Only on one occasion I got caught. When I think of it now, here in Australia, I blush, and am horrified at my younger self.

Two days before my 16th birthday I was caught driving a noisy trail motorbike (an Aprilia 50 cc) in the wrong direction of a one-way street in the historic centre of Antwerp, with my girlfriend from school on the back. Neither of us were wearing helmets; we just wanted to visit Antwerp and buy some schoolbooks. The police impounded my motorbike, and later that day released it after my mother had personally pleaded with the Mayor of Antwerp. I got away with it.

What is the current project you are working on?

I have a big solo exhibition coming up at Mundaring Arts Centre called 'Tributaries', 5 Nov - 19 December 2021. This was postponed from April 2020 due to COVID-19.

My current writing project is *When Tom was Tommo*. It is inspired by the work I was doing in victim and offender mediation. It is a fiction story set in Western Australia about someone who has spent most of his life in prison and now wants to turn his life around and start a family.

I started writing it in 2016, took time for research, took a break, and I am now in my second draft.

CHAPTER 5

JASON CHATFIELD
(Internationally syndicated cartoonist/ Stand up comedian)

Jason Chatfield
Credit: Jason Chatfield

PROFILE

Born in 1984 Jason Chatfield is an Australian cartoonist and stand-up comedian, now based in New York City.

In 2007 he took over writing and drawing the iconic internationally syndicated comic strip Ginger Meggs. This made him the strips fifth artist, succeeding James Kemsley. Kemsley wrote to the Bancks family to secure approval for Chatfield to succeed him. Thus at 23 he became Australia's most widely syndicated cartoonist, appearing daily in over 120 newspapers in 34 countries.

At 26 he was elected president of the Australian Cartoonists' Association, making him the youngest person to hold the position since the organisation began in 1924. He currently serves as President of the National Cartoonists Society (est. 1946).

Chatfield's art spans the disciplines of comic strip, gag cartoon, editorial cartoon, book illustration, caricature and commercial art. His would has appeared in *The New Yorker* and Mad magazine. To find out more and see his range of books go to www.jasonchatfield.com.

Instagram @jasonchatfield

INTERVIEW

Apart from family, what were your greatest one or two achievements?

Getting published in *The New Yorker* was a long and arduous journey... that's a big one. That, and taking over Ginger Meggs.

How did you come to live this type of life?

I think I always had in the back of my head subconsciously that I would like to be in New York working as an artist. It is the place most conducive to creativity of anywhere else I have ever been. Paris is a close second.

How do you think the life you've lived is different from others?

I don't think it's any more or less interesting. I find everybody's lives interesting. They are all stories and a series of habits, decisions and personality traits that make everyone different.

What was your biggest challenge in achieving your goals or getting to where you are now?

Jealous critics within the industry, and editors with poor judgement.

The lack of foresight of newspaper editors has led to so few great ideas in cartooning taking off. The cartoonists have had to fly off without the editors, since editors have typically been so slow to adapt to the changing landscape.

The critics who go out of their way to pull you and your work apart are projecting insecurities of their own. But it doesn't make it any easier to plough through when they keep tugging at your ankles when you're trying to innovate.

How often have you thought about giving up?

Never. I just couldn't picture myself doing anything else.

What have you learnt from any difficulties or failures along the way?

To trust my gut. To plan ahead.

To treat my future self well, as if they're a different person.

When Preparation Meets Opportunity has been the biggest reason for nearly every success I've had.

Create for yourself. The people who like it will find you. Those who don't will fall away. You'll be left with a loyal core of people who like what you're doing.

Don't curate your art to what gets likes. Curate it to what you like.

Money isn't everything. Never stop drawing for yourself.

What motivates or drives you?

Coffee. And a striving to get better every day. But mainly coffee.

What else helped you get to where you are?

Honestly, I think it is the ability to ask questions of peers and mentors. I don't think I'd be anywhere near where I am today without the generous help of mentors and colleagues who were able to point me in the right direction when I didn't know where to start, or where to go next. The ability to communicate with your community of artists is invaluable.

What main message(s) or advice would you give others?

Never stop learning.

Try new things all the time, and always prioritise time for your health. You can't create anything without it.

Has planning or goal setting been part of your process?

I have a planning session every October for the year ahead, and I track everything in a BuJo.

I can't stress enough how important planning ahead is if you want to achieve anything; life will get in the way. That's guaranteed. But if you have a structure to fall back on, to keep incrementally growing and moving towards the thing you want, you'll never lose momentum.

I think the key also is to surround yourself with other people to whom you're accountable, but who won't judge if your direction shifts and you pursue new opportunities when they present themselves.

Growing up, to what extent did you feel different from your peers?

A lot.

I never really fitted in with the popular kids. I kept to myself and drew all the time. I buried myself in my drawing. It's all I ever did. I only had a couple of close friends as a kid.

To what extent did you feel you fitted into society when you were growing up? (5 is didn't fit in, 1 easy fitted in).

Score 4.

I always felt just outside of everything that was happening. I've never felt that I've been part of the big mainstream in any sense. I'm an introvert and I like my solitude. Strange for a comedian I know, but it tracks if you ask any other comedian.

If the Police listed you as a person of interest what would it be for?

Probably for letting my dog pee somewhere illegal.

What is the current project you are working on?

I'm really excited about a new series I'm working on called *Creatures of New York*. It's a series of drawings and stories collected over the span of 5 years in Manhattan that we're creating a book out of. The NYC Link program will be showing it around the city on their 40,000 digital LCD screens on street corners in Manhattan.

New books include:

Ginger Meggs (to celebrate 100 years of this iconic character)

Covid Chronicles: A Comic Anthology (more than 60 short comics from various artists).

CHAPTER 6

MEGAN SIMPSON HUBERMAN (Film Director/Developer/Writer)

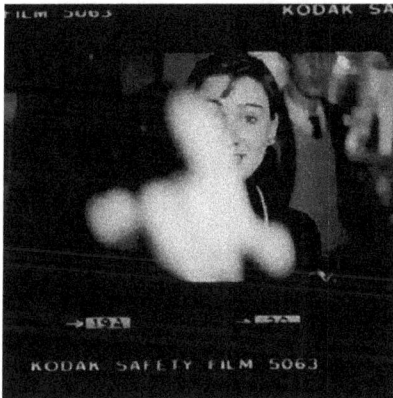

Megan Simpson Huberman
Credit: Anne Sconberg

PROFILE

Megan Simpson Huberman is a writer, director, development consultant, script editor, story producer, and senior development/ production/ creative executive in the Australian screen industry.

She has written, directed and developed feature films, TV drama, comedy and documentary, and worked with hundreds of writers, directors and producers across Australia.

A directing graduate of the Australian and French film schools, Simpson Huberman has a thirty-year career in the film and television industry. She's known for warm, appealing and accessible storytelling. She works across Australia and Asia. Recent projects include the highly successful series *KL Gangster: Underworld* for iflix Malaysia, one of the most ambitious TV dramas in the country's history. She works extensively in TV drama writer's rooms and has expertise in supporting new writers.

She is currently writer and co-creator of the miniseries *Goolagong*, in development with ABC TV. She is also writing the feature adaptation *The Secret Lives Of Dresses*, in development with Universal.

Simpson Huberman has held major executive roles in the screen industry, including Director of Development and Production Investment at Screen NSW, Development Executive at ScreenAustralia and Director of the Indivision ProjectLab at the Australian Film Commission. Features that she has backed have been selected for Cannes, Venice, Berlin and Toronto.

Dating The Enemy, her second feature (starring Guy Pearce), which she wrote and directed, was a significant box office success in Australia, where it attracted a huge following and became one of the highest rating movies of the year on network television subsequent to its theatre release. The film garnered an Australian Film Institute Best Actress nomination of its female lead, Claudia Karvan.

Alex, her first feature after graduating from Australian and French Film schools, screened in competition at the Toronto Film Festival.

In 2015 she wrote and was attached to direct the feature adaptation of *Salvation Creek*, based on the bestselling memoir published by Random House, to be distributed by Paramount, with finance approved from ScreenAustralia.

She has run Aurora, the southern hemisphere's premium feature film script development workshop; and she is a member of the Australian Directors' Guild Women in Film Action Committee. This committee helped launch the Gender Matters initiative in Australia.

Simpson Huberman has three degrees from three film schools.

Instagram @meganshhhhhh

INTERVIEW

Apart from family, what were your greatest one or two achievements?

When I was a screen executive, a team of producers brought in a feature film project with a young female writer director who had never directed a frame of film before. The script was dark and disturbing, and some people were vehemently opposed to it being supported. I thought she had a voice and that the story was distinct and deserved being made, so I backed it. The film went on to be the first Australian film for a decade to be selected for Main Competition at the Cannes Film Festival, and sold out every territory.

As a writer, I have been working for 3 years now on developing a miniseries on the great Australian female indigenous tennis champion Evonne Goolagong. I want our culture to see more stories of female heroes. I hope it will be produced next year, and if so, I will be very proud of it.

How do you think the life you've lived is from others?

I've been in the film and TV industry since I was 16 years old really. I have worked across writing, developing, script editing, TV drama rooms, financing, talent development, and industry development, in Australia and internationally.

I've travelled to film festivals and markets, worked with creative people, worked with governments, had my films screened in cinemas and on TV. In developing stories for the screen, I tried to understand the human soul and my own.

How did you come to live this type of life?

I always thought I would write novels. But when I was 15 years old I decided that the screen was the medium for our era. So I went and did an adult evening film and TV course at FTI in Fremantle. From there I decided that I wanted to work in film & TV.

My parents were worried that I should do law instead, but my high school English literature teacher Mrs Rita Lynn persuaded them that it was a growing area and that they should support me.

Have you missed out on anything by living this type of life?

I'm not as rich as I might have been if I had gone into another area of business. But I am comfortable, and I enjoy my life.

How often have you thought about giving up?

A few times.

What was your biggest challenge in achieving your goals or getting to where you are now?

Though talent is important, interpersonal skills are also crucial.

As a slightly shy nerd with definite ideas about things, I have had to work on my collaborative and social skills.

As a screen executive, I saw many talented directors fail because of their poor collaborative skills.

You need to have a vision BUT be able to share your vision and open it up for others to feed into it.

As I work both as a writer and as a script editor helping other writers, I have learned that the best work comes from being open to good ideas from your trusted partners. That dance, between vision and collaboration, is the heart of the creative conundrum for screen projects.

I am both confident and shy. I have achieved many things, but also have doubts.

What have you learnt from any difficulties or failures along the way?

Collaboration. Reworking. Emotional insight.

I have a creative mentor, the US screenwriter Meg Lefauve, who has taught me that when writing the writer's subconscious often hides the most crucial thing from them, because it is the most painful.

You have to persist and keep working for that crucial insight and emotional depth to be gradually revealed.

I took 12 years out of my own writing and directing to work as a screen executive helping others get their projects made, while my daughter was in school. It has definitely been a challenge re-starting my own creative career in my 50's, and sometimes I have wondered if I have left my second run too late. But it has also been incredibly creatively satisfying.

I give myself interim goals, tell myself each year that I will back myself creatively for the year ahead and then reassess. My projects are moving ahead and my CV continues to grow, as do my skills.

What motivates or drives you?

I am in love with story.

It's like emotional detective work. It's endlessly fascinating and compelling.

What else helped you get to where you are?

I am hard working, persistent, compelling, analytical, but also in touch with my emotions.

I often cry when reading a script or pitching an idea in a story room. My emotions and my life experience as a woman my age are my superpowers. I have a lot of emotional experience to bring to stories.

I am also always ready to learn.

And the older I get the better I get at listening to my creative instincts.

Has planning or goal setting been part of your process?

Because I am a freelancer and work from home a lot, I need to have timelines and delivery dates and working time all plotted in my diary.

Even though I am experienced I am still shy about putting myself forward for projects, so I do try to set some annual goals and challenges for myself, and this has been very productive.

What main message(s) or advice would you give others?

I'd say that talent makes up 40% and collaboration is 60%.

Growing up, to what extent did you feel different from your peers?

A lot.

I'm a shy nerd! I can be a good public speaker and confident when I am advocating for others, but I am still shy and sensitive.

When I was growing up, I loved to read and write stories so I was often in my own head, and I was skipped ahead a year in primary school (because I had already finished the next year's work) so I was a little behind the social eight ball. But I had a few good friends who were wonderful. We weren't the cool kids, and we weren't the total dags, we were nice smart kids in the middle and that was great.

To what extent did you feel you fitted into society when you were growing up? (5 is felt on the outside, 1 easy fitted in).

Middle of the road. Score of 3. See previous.

If the police listed you as a person of interest what would it be for?

If the police interviewed me as a person of interest it would NOT be as a witness to an accident on a film set - because I am very, very serious about on set safety for cast and crew!

What is the current project?

The mini series about the great Australian female indigenous tennis champion Evonne Goolagong. It's currently in development with ABC TV drama.

CHAPTER 7

NEIL RAWLINS (Travel Photographer/Writer/ Guide)

Neil Rawlins
Credit: Neil Rawlins

PROFILE

Neil Rawlins has spent 50 years travelling the globe both on personal expeditions, including 40 years as a professional tour guide, tour operator, travel photographer and writer. His experiences have been captured through stunning photography and witty penmanship. These experiences map present day travel, back to a time when plane travel was a once in a lifetime experience for the average man. A time of hitch-hiking, telegrams and landline telephones, if you were lucky.

Growing up in Te Atatu, a suburb of Auckland, and attending Rutherford High School during the 1960's, he left school at 17. His working career began as a clerical worker with the Department of Lands and Survey in Auckland, before moving on to Air New Zealand, a move largely taken for its concession flights.

His first overseas excursion was on the MV *Tofua* which was known affectionately as the banana boat. The trip visited the Pacific islands of Fiji, Samoa, American Samoa, Niue and Tonga.

Armed with a passion for photography, and a film camera he set about capturing his adventures. It should be remembered that this was a time of film rolls that required developing, not digital methods where you could snap off several shots and delete the unwanted ones. It could be weeks before you saw the photographic results, and then you had to remember where the photos were taken!

In February 1970 he set off, first to Singapore (using his Air New Zealand staff flight concession) then on to Kathmandu where he joined a Penn Overland journey across Asia to London.

While in Britain he worked in a number of seasonal jobs, particularly in the agricultural section and regularly went grape picking in France.

In June 1971 he took a tour to Scandinavia and the USSR, and travelled independently in France, Spain and Morocco.

Three years later he embarked on an Overland truck trip from London to Nairobi, across the Sahara and through Central Africa.

He then hitch-hiked south to Johannesburg, where he worked for Kentucky Fried Chicken for a few months, before hitch-hiking back up to Zimbabwe (then Rhodesia), Mozambique (then Portuguese) and through South Africa where he caught the *Fairsky* back to New Zealand, via Australia.

In New Zealand he found work as a livestock officer with the Department of Agriculture in Dargaville, but soon became unsettled.

Around three years later he set off to the USA where he worked the best part of a year in Wyoming on an exploratory drilling rig looking for uranium. He then headed across to London once again.

In March 1979 he went on the Sundowners training trip and became a tour leader. After many years of exploring the globe he'd found his vocation at last.

The 1980's saw the beginning of several technological improvements that would make international travel far easier, but it wasn't until the end of the decade that they started to become a reality. The mobile phone and digital cameras were still over 10 years away.

During this time he undertook several Overland tours to India & Nepal, but also into the Middle East, to Egypt and Europe.

When the company folded in 1982, he moved to Explore Worldwide, another UK tour operator. There he ran their camel safaris in Rajasthan which required a whole new set of skills. More importantly though it was there that he met his partner Jan.

Whilst at Explore Worldwide he took tours up to Kashmir and Ladakh, to Petra and the Desert Castles of Jordan, through Aegean Turkey, to Tunisia and also to Nepal, Darjeeling and Sikkim.

In 1985 the couple married in England and decided to return to New Zealand. A year later they set up the Antipodean Explorer tour company.

At first they ran day trips out of Auckland, then took on the Explore Worldwide contract for their tours in New Zealand. Their company prospered for 17 years, a great achievement in the travel industry.

Approaching retirement age and after a dalliance with cancer, he continued contracting to various US and UK companies as a tour leader. It seemed nothing could stop his adventurous spirit, and then Covid came along.

Not one to sit still, he has been driving the 'Sugar Train' around the Chelsea Sugar Refinery 3-4 days a week.

We can be extremely thankful that he decided to share his many adventures and insights through his travel blog and travel books. Through these we can remember a time when international travel was a true adventure, and stunning photography took more than just many clicks and filters.

Travel blog Dust On My Feet www.neilrawlins.blogspot.com
Instagram @dustonmyfeet and @antipodeanneil
Books: Amazon under Neil Stanley Rawlins:
One Foot In Front Of The Other: First Steps
One Foot In Front Of The Other: Full Stride
Stone From Anzac Cove and Other Travel Tales.

INTERVIEW

How did you come to live this type of life?

I guess I always wanted to travel. My ancestral family, on my mother's side, had been early colonial adventurers and dad had come out to New Zealand as a child just after World War 1.

Mum had both Maori and Polynesian (Wallis Island) ancestry. Her great grandfather was John Milsome Jury, a sailor who jumped ship (from a whaler) in the Bay of Islands, and was the patriarch of the well-known, and large, Jury family of the Wairarapa. He had married Te Aitu-o-te-Rangi, daughter of the Maori chief Whatahoro, who was killed by Te Rauparaha's men during the Musket Wars.

Mum's paternal grandfather, George Edgerton Westbrook was a well-known trader in Samoa, and before that in many of the smaller islands in the Pacific. He married a Wallis Islander and that is where my maternal grandfather was born.

So I guess it wasn't unusual that a sense of adventure was in my blood.

Mum's older brother saw the Second World War as an adventure and kept a diary of the campaigns in Greece and Crete, but he was killed during the Battle of Sidi Rezegh in 1941. I have his diary and the last entry in the evening before he was killed – *"subject of a future book"*!

My first lengthy overseas experience began with an Overland journey from Kathmandu in Nepal, through India, Pakistan, Afghanistan, Iran & Turkey to Europe. This was followed by a period working and travelling in Britain, Europe and the former Soviet Union, before returning through Africa. I initially travelled by truck from London to Nairobi, I then hitch-hiked down to Jo'burg and eventually Cape Town from where I caught a ship home.

My second lengthy overseas experience began almost 4 years later when I travelled first to USA. Then back to London where I took up a position as a tour leader. This meant taking tours on the Overland routes between London and Kathmandu. Later I went on to run Camel Safaris in Rajasthan and special interest tours in Kashmir/Ladakh, Jordan, Turkey and elsewhere before returning to New Zealand.

Since then, I have continued in the travel industry leading tours in New Zealand and Australia.

What do you consider to be your greatest one or two achievements? (apart from family).

Being accepted and becoming a tour leader (courier) on the London to Kathmandu Overland routes in the late 1970's.

What was your biggest challenge in achieving your goals?

When I was young I was always very shy. Perhaps the biggest hurdle I had to overcome was having the confidence to speak in front of a group of people. The first time I did this was at a wedding where I was best man. A number of people, including my parents were surprised.

The Sundowner's European training trip, which I had to go on before I was accepted as a tour leader, helped build my confidence immensely, especially when I realised that other prospective tour leaders were like myself, or worse!

Along the way did you ever think about giving up?

As a tour guide - never.

Being a tour leader is always rewarding. But as you are dealing a lot with human nature, there can always be unknowns. There are barriers or set-backs, but these can generally be overcome relatively easily and with patience. I guess there are always moments, as with any work, that you start thinking "What am I doing this for?" Then good times happen.

What have you learnt from any difficulties or failures along the way?

You definitely learn how to overcome problems and setbacks.

This was before the days of modern communications. At best, we may have found a phone or a telex in larger town, but we would normally have to book 'air' time. Telegrams were the instant media in those days. They may have got through reasonably quickly, but then you had to wait for a reply – always reliant on local opening hours!

As we were often in remote areas, we soon learnt how to be re-sourceful. You also had to learn patience. If you became impatient, particularly with border officials, you could end up being delayed for twice as long as you need be.

What kept/keeps you going? What is driving you?

The sense of adventure.

The idea of going places, meeting people. Even just doing regular day tours, there was always this appeal.

Ever since I was a youngster growing up in a then isolated New Zealand, I knew I wanted to travel. My primary school teacher told me he had been to 50 countries and in 1960, I thought this was amazing.

My first trip away from New Zealand was on the 'Tofua', the old banana-boat which visited some of the South Pacific Islands once a month, to take up necessary supplies and bring back bananas and co-pra. In those days the ship was the only regular contact some of these islands (Niue, Vava'u) had with the outside world.

What else helped you get to where you are?

Having an enquiring mind.

When you are dealing with different nationalities and religions, having at least some rudimentary knowledge helps immensely, and immediately establishes credibility and a rapport.

And now of course I am supported in my writing endeavours by my wife, Jan.

What, if anything, do you feel you've missed out on by living this type of life?

Probably the security of a settled lifestyle with strong local connections.

And an accumulation of wealth, but then I knew this was a sacrifice I was prepared to make when I became a professional tour leader, as tour work does tend to be seasonal. Initially I never thought this would last for most of my life, but it has.

What's your attitude to planning and goal setting?

Planning, and setting a goal in the travel industry has always been difficult, especially with limited financial backing and with the ever-changing political climates and now with Covid lockdowns.

My goal now is to have my books and photographs published, as a legacy on what has now become a past era.

What main message(s) or advice would you give others thinking about living a life outside the norm?

Think carefully.
Follow your heart.

Growing up, to what extent did you feel different from your peers?

1 easily fitted in.
I always fitted in, joined in with work colleagues when I was growing up. Fun times with many a serious hangover!! Certainly, times that I look back on fondly.

If the Police listed you as a person of interest what would it be for?

Probably because I have visited a number of what would now be classified as 'dodgy' countries *viz.* Afghanistan, Iran, Iraq.
When I was working in South Africa, I was labelled a Communist by a fellow Afrikaans worker because I told him I had visited the USSR!!

What is the current project you're working on?

My writing in my *On Foot in Front of the Other* books reflects my experiences travelling, both privately and as a tour guide. I am currently revising and expanding the first two books of my travels:

One Foot In Front Of The Other: First Steps
One Foot In Front Of The Other: Full Stride

These books are currently on Amazon ebooks along with *A Stone From Anzac Cove and Other Travel Tales.*

I aim to complete a third book in the *One Foot In Front of The Other series* which will be *Stepping Back.* Hopefully finding a mainstream publisher who can do justice to my photos. Maybe coffee table style books could follow?

CHAPTER 8

CHRIS MORGAN
(Fastest Australian With MS On a Motorbike

Chris Morgan
Credit: Chris Morgan

PROFILE

Chris Morgan began his working life as a boilermaker and progressed onto welding, after attaining certificates from the Welding Institute of Australia. Two decades of extremely hard work saw him reach the top of his craft, obtaining the highest code recognised in the world. Hardly surprising then, that a few years later he found himself packing up his life in Victoria to work as a Leading Hand Special Class Welder, on a highly sought-after Barrow Island job.

Life was on track. He'd reached the top of his profession and established a solid reputation. He had a nice apartment, wonderful partner, and several big boy toys to play with.

In 2008 he and his partner bought a caravan and set out to explore Australia. The adventure lasted 18 months and brought him to Western Australia where he took on a special class welding job.

Welding in 50 degrees heat requires a steady hand but also a strong mental fortitude, something he'd have to rely on once the diagnosis came.

Initially Morgan noticed he was getting fatigued quicker at work. He put it down to working long hours in extreme heat, but then he started tripping over more often. He could no longer hide the issue.

A visit to the doctor started a barrage of tests which ended with a diagnosis of Multiple Sclerosis in September 2016.

Since then, he has gone on to become the Fastest Australian with MS on a motorbike over a quarter mile. He has also returned to full time work.

INTERVIEW

Apart from family, what were your greatest one or two achievements?

Being able to get back to work four years after my diagnosis and doing a full day's work in a physical job that has me on my feet all day. After my diagnosis I had to give up my welding career. I found this really hard and wondered if that was it. But by working hard and not giving up I've been able to return to work.

For the motorbike racing, with my bike we've proved that even with MS you can race a motorbike, and now I know there are people who will help.

I guess another thing is, just trying hard to be a good person.

How did you come to live this type of life?

In my twenties I wasn't that happy, it could have been undiagnosed depression, I guess. But I'm stubborn. I went back to school and got a good job that paid well, and I started to think better about myself.

After my diagnosis I was told to go on medication, something I initially delayed doing. I was also referred to the MSWA Physiotherapy Department for assessment.

Three months after the diagnosis I joined the MSWA Physiotherapy Department's Wednesday night gym class. Every week I took part in 40 minutes gym work, followed by another 40 minutes in the pool. Aside from exercising, the MSWA gym also provided a tightknit social group where anything was up for discussion. The social outlet was a bonus as I'd had to give up work.

For the racing, I have always been interested in racing. When I was younger I used to have a drag racing car, but I didn't have the money to race it.

What motivates or drives you?

I guess it started with watching my mum die of cancer when I was 30 years old. That made me want to do something before it was all too late.

Also, while I saw people looking for money making schemes, my grandad taught me that the only way to get money was to get a job and work hard. I learnt that no one is going to do it for you, you have to do it yourself.

In terms of the MS, the friendship gained at the MSWA gym motivated me to take part in the 2017 Ocean Ride, where I raised over $1,000 for the organisation. I enjoyed it so much I did it again the following year.

Six months after my first Ocean Ride, two years after my diagnosis, I arrived at the 2018 MSWA Step Up challenge. Initially I'd planned to watch the MSWA Physiotherapy team climb over 1,000 steps to the top of one of Perth's tallest buildings. However, I woke up wanting to challenge myself, and decided to join in. When I started up the steps, I thought I'd show them up (ha ha). I eventually got on top of the roof. Last man out but I did it and everyone was so happy for me.

Around this time, I began finding it difficult to ride my motorbike on the road. I'd dropped my motorbike a couple of times at the traffic lights. So, I started a discussion with Wayne and Todd Patterson, of Wayne Patterson's Motorcycle Centre, a Ducati Dealer in Bunbury. They said I could still ride a motorbike and suggested they help me begin my motorbike racing career, by building a special head turning Ducati Race Bike at the dealership.

Wayne said to me "Let's build it. Let's prove that someone with MS can ride a motorbike."

That was all the encouragement I needed, and soon the dream started. I wanted to race in the WA Drag Race Season. Then I started to think I'd like to be the fastest man on a motorbike with MS. I kept it to myself for a long time, then started telling some close friends.

I have a good bunch of people at the track who treat me like normal. They make me feel accepted. And the support soon went beyond the immediate team to other people at the track. It must look funny, they see this guy struggling to walk and they ask if he needs help, then he gets on the motorbike.

At home my long-term partner Ebony Briggs started to feel less concerned too. She was worried about me hurting himself and setting back all my hard work. But once she was there at the track, she was relieved at the great family who supported me. Track officials and other competitors were coming up to her saying how awesome it was that I was having a crack and doing so well.

Away from the track other differences were occurring. People noticed that my walking had improved, and I had no interest in riding my motorbike on the road, no interest in hooning around ... it's safer on the track.

More interesting though were the emotional changes. It's changed my life. There were some dark times, but this has taken my mind off all the crap. Things are not as bad as they seem, it's given me an outlet. I believe in myself again. Ebony also saw the changes. She could see I was having so much fun. She said she could feel my excitement and hear it in my voice.

What else helped you get to where you are?

I couldn't have done it without the help of Wayne and Todd Patterson and the guys at Wayne Patterson's Motorcycle Centre. Also the guys at Star Physio helped me rebuild lost muscle and increase my physical fitness. Plus my sponsors Bunbury Dyno who took a chance on me.

I need to mention my partner Ebony, who supported me though all the hard work, and all the other friends who supported me, even if it was just a short message of encouragement on Instagram. All those messages really helped.

Has planning or goal setting been part of your process?

I don't know about planning. I have been a bit of an opportunist at time. But then I've always been ready and felt the need to keep achieving and not to plateaux. Probably goes back to what I said about my mum.

For the Step Up, there was no planning. I just woke up feeling like a challenge.

For the motorbike racing, definitely, yes lots of planning. Initially my goal was to finish in the top ten and more importantly have heaps of fun. Secretly though, I thought about being the fastest man with MS on the drag strip.

It took twelve months to build the bike, during which I added in more physiotherapy sessions, this time at Star Physio. They designed a program of squats and deadlifts concentrating on good technique over heavy weights. The program started with 20 kilogram single leg presses (80 kilos with two legs). Working out twice a week, to reduce fatigue, I was soon amazed that I could press 102 kilos with one leg (280k two legs).

Soon another sponsor came on board, Bunbury Dyno.

By October 2018 the bike had arrived, and we were ready for my first run. Initially my times were inconsistent, with an average of 11.7 seconds at 207km per hour.

During the next race meeting we made it into the first-round elimination, and after five races we were consistently clocking personal best times. The time was down to 11.04 seconds at 212 km.

By February 2019 we'd achieved 10.81. and had our first race win. My main problem was not riding down the straight but leaping out too early at the start lights. By March at the *48th Western Nationals*, our personal best time was down to 10.51 seconds. By the end of the year I was stoked when I was announced *Rookie Rider of the Year*.

After that I've been concentrating on improving my times, my reaction time at the start, and being more consistent.

The next goal was to get back to work. I wanted to test myself, to see how I would go in terms of fatigue, the heat and being on my feet. We smashed it. I'm working a full day, three and a half days a week, on my feet all day walking around a lot and in all sorts of weather. It only took four years (laughing). I went into the interview and said to the guy "I'm doing this for my own reasons, I need to test myself to see what I can do", and he took me on.

How often have you thought about giving up?

Not much. After my diagnosis there was a lot of uncertainty. There was a loss of career, I thought what am I doing to do workwise? But then I thought I can't not, not work.

You just have to get on with it don't you? There's no point giving up.

I was given a plaque by my Grade 2 school teacher that said "if you think you can, you can, life's battles are not always won by the fastest or the strongest. If you think you can, you can." That has stayed with me ever since and is almost like a mantra for me.

What have you learnt from any difficulties or failures along the way?

With MS I learnt you get out of it what you put in. You could sit on your arse and get worse or go to the gym and try to improve. I wasn't a gym person before this so I wasn't sure, but I went and I started seeing improvements.

I learnt I'm quite a strong person. That no matter how hard you get knocked down you can learn from it and continue to move forward. It's important to keep active both mentally and physically. To keep using your skills or you will lose them.

Through Drag racing I learnt to change one thing and then check to see what difference it makes. We do that with the motorbike. It might be a slow process but that way you learn which bits work. You can do the same with your health.

One of the most surprising aspects was the amount of support forming around me.

To what extent did you feel you fitted into society when you were growing up? (5 is felt on the outside, 1 easy fitted in).

5/5 not at all.

I was different. I had dyslexia and couldn't spell at school. At primary school they wanted us to learn Italian and at high school, Japanese. I was struggling with English.

But I liked not fitting in. I liked being an individual. I was picked on, and they put labels on me but that's a good thing. I see it as more of an asset, it makes you stand out from the crowd.

I don't like the idea of "you must do this. You must buy a new iPhone, be materialistic". There's more to life than that.

I liked that when I had money to go to a posh restaurant, and I could go in my jeans if I wanted to.

What main message(s) or advice would you give others?

I'd say put in the effort. You don't have to be a Rhode Scholar or be wealthy to do you what you want to do. If you want to do something do it.

Don't listen to the knockers, it's easy to knock someone. Unfortunately, we have social jealously especially in Australia with the tall poppy thing where they want to tear you down. It can be hard to do but put it aside and focus on what you want to achieve.

Find the right people to support you.

Most importantly have a crack.

If the Police listed you as a person of interest what would it be for?

For being a bit of a weirdo. For being different, not a conformist. For not working for the man or fitting the norm.

What is the current project you are working on?

With my past career I'd like to become a trainer or assessor to pass on my knowledge.

With the motorbike it's about consistency in my results.

I'd also like to find a way to use my experience to help others, especially young people get through tough times.

CHAPTER 9

FRANCES MABER OBE
(Wildlife Educator/First Female State Director Commonwealth Public Service Dept.)

Frances Maber
Credit: Frances Maber

PROFILE

Frances Maber has been a children's book writer since 2006.

Maber's writing comes from a solid base in education as demonstrated by her being awarded an OBE in 1979 for services to education.

After 6 years of teaching Maber left the profession to join the public service. She was the first woman promoted to a position of State Director of a Commonwealth Public Service Department. She held the role for 10 years in Western Australia and a further 3 years in Victorian Commonwealth Department of Education. She became the second woman appointed as a University Registrar.

Her children's book writing focuses on bush fantasy. However, her background in education ensures her books are grounded in scientific fact about each character.

Her main character is Willit, a Northern Hairy Nosed Wombat, a sub-species that is seriously endangered. Proceeds from the children's books goes to the Wombat Foundation for the care of Northern Hairy Nosed Wombats.

Through the tales Maber reveals the lifecycle and the lifestyle of wombats, including natural dangers, food sources and burrow architecture. Human intervention is virtually absent.

Willit appears in three books *Willit's Friends, Willit the Wombat Grows Up* and *Willit the Amazing Wombat.* Willit also has his own website and Facebook page. Copies of his books can be found in primary schools across Western Australia.

Willit has friends in many parts of the world. In 2014 he wrote to the Socceroos congratulating them on choosing Nutmeg the wombat as their mascot. He pointed out the many similarities between wombats and soccer players. This letter was shared with all the teams in the competition. As a result, his Facebook page collected friends from China and many other countries. As a corollary, in 2018 a colour-in book *Colour Willit's Walkabout* was produced. It ends with Willit seeing a Panda.

Other books include *Bush Surprises* (2015) a collection of 26 poems each about an aspect of the bush, as well as *Bush Christmas* (2017) an old man's celebrations.

www.willitthewombat.com

INTERVIEW

Apart from family, what were your greatest one or two achievements?

Two Chinese children living in Sydney asked if they might translate *Willit's Friends* (the first book of the series), which they have done. I'm still working with them on how to print and distribute the book further. It's an exciting time and I am learning a lot, talking to printers, lawyers etc.

How do you think the life you've lived is different from others?

That is a mystery.

How did you come to live this type of life?

My passion from about age 10 to 28 years of age was to be a singer. It influenced my life until I was 28 when I knew it wasn't going to happen. My Perth reputation was good, but La Scala wasn't going to happen! Singing at that time was a pastime not a passion.

I was 27 when I left teaching for the Commonwealth Public Service. Getting that job had elements of "fluke". It was a very different working environment. During that time I became consciously Australian and interested in how politics works.

As a writer I had written tales for child relatives, but when a drive through forest in Victoria revealed the full horror of wombat roadkill, I decided to write about it honestly for children. The topic was researched, and my writing style changed until the first story was ready for a publisher. They weren't interested.

Self-publishing was another learning experience. With the help of an amazing artist (Alexander Hills) I produced 6 beautifully illustrated books each, in its own way, faithfully depicting truths about the Australian bush.

Writing for adults came next.

The thought of a family memoir for my husband emerged in 1975. Research was completed by 1992 but how best to use it? *Remembering Catharine* is an imaginary biography of my husband's great great grandmother. It was published in 2019 by Linellen Press and is available as paperback or e-book through Amazon or from the publisher.

What was your biggest challenge in achieving your goals or getting to where you are now?

In terms of writing for adults, it was constantly shelving projects, as first wombats and then family took precedence.

Most of my friends and family thought it an unlikely thing to spend time on.

How often have you thought about giving up?

In my working life, hardly never.

I led a charmed life, respected by subordinate staff (who wanted me to get the jobs), by contacts outside my Department and my colleagues in other States and in Canberra. I took on any new project suggested, this despite unequal pay for several years.

In terms of writing, I thought about giving up a few times when trying to complete my first novel. The urge to discover the adult fiction story hit in 1991.

What have you learnt from any difficulties or failures along the way?

If you want to ask a question, then do. Many times (especially in the singing world) I didn't speak up.

When I retired and started writing I could have found help from groups, but I failed to 'seek and find'.

What motivates or drives you?

At work, knowledge that the Department's policies were valuable in terms of giving more opportunities for education for more people.

Personally, stubbornness. I can do this.

In terms of the adult novel, a desire to finish something that my husband would have enjoyed.

What else helped you get to where you are?

My husband's unfailing support and more recently a small group of real friends.

Has planning or goal setting been part of your process?

The children's books are not planned. They emerged from facts gathered haphazardly.

Remembering Catharine was planned in detail from documents and via exploration of the main locations.

What main message(s) or advice would you give others?

If you believe in something you want to do, achieve, or be, then don't be put off by family or friends "advice".

Trust your instinct.

To what extent did you feel you fitted into society when you were growing up?

Middle of the road to a little on the outside.

I was shy with new people and silent in group discussions. I was not pushy to establish my place in a group.

I never learnt to network.

If the police listed you as a person of interest what would it be for?

No idea. What about scaring passengers in my car.

What is the current project you are working on?

Another novel, the probable title is *Village Harmonics*. The novel is set in England in late 2015-early 2017. I've been working on it and been stirred on by two people who have read bits. I am making it less charming all the time. I applied to Australian Society of Authors (ASA) for a "mentor grant" but with 20 grants and 200 applicants, I didn't rate. I kept working and toughening the line.

A while after that I wrote to ASA and asked for help in finding a mentor indicating that I could afford to pay. Much to my delight I got a quick reply with three suggestions, advice on how to go forward and what material I'd need for the next step. That sharpened my mind no end because I need a full manuscript as well as the first 10 pages etc. I have a lot of work to do to get that finished.

However, the novel had too many flaws and *Catharine* was in my head, so it went in the cupboard until *Remembering Catharine* was safely with the publisher.

It's still in the cupboard and now I'm working on my memoir based on 24 years in the Commonwealth Public Service.

CHAPTER 10

DR SARAH GILES
(Family/Humanitarian Physician)

Dr Sarah Giles
Dr Sarah Giles

PROFILE

Dr Sarah Giles is a Canadian trained family, emergency, humanitarian physician who works mostly in remote and rural communities in northern Canada, Western Australia, and conflict zones. She has undertaken five assignments with Médecins Sans Frontier.

As an example of her work, she has worked on Christmas Island during a horrific boat crash in 2010.

She was on MSF's ship Aquarius in the Mediterranean doing search and rescue in 2016. As the doctor on board, she provided care to the passengers many of whom had been on the road for months, fleeing terrible conditions in their home countries.

When the sea is too rough for smugglers to launch boats, she can be found swabbing the decks and working on her French and Arabic language skills.

She believes "we need to find diplomatic ways to allow people to seek asylum rather than pushing them out to sea to drown". #SafePassage

Giles is also a freelance journalist, an advocate for universal single payer health care, and a dog lover.

Her lifestyle means she often has no fixed address.

Twitter: @SarahGiles10

www.blogs.msf.org/bloggers/sarah-giles

INTERVIEW

Apart from family, what were your greatest one or two achievements?

Cobbling together an unconventional life that I love and find challenging.
Maintaining sustained moral outrage in the face of inequality.

How do you think the life you've lived is different from others?

While my mailing address is my sister's house in Ottawa, Canada, I'm rarely there. I travel a ton for work, volunteering, and pleasure.
Many people couldn't cope with being away from home for such long periods of time. But my sister creates the world's most supportive environment and encourages me to get out there. I couldn't live my life this way without her.
I'm also not a huge consumer of "things". My lack of the need to have the latest thing (other than books) keeps my life affordable.

What was your biggest challenge in achieving your goals or getting to where you are now?

Imposter syndrome.
My refusal to say what people want to hear.

How often have you thought about giving up?

A few times.
I don't tend to do things the easy way. But, to steal a line from Jane Austen ...

"There is a stubbornness about me that never can bear to be frightened at the will of others. My courage always rises at every attempt to intimidate me."

What have you learnt from any difficulties or failures along the way?

Sometimes you catch more flies with honey.

What motivates or drives you?

I firmly believe that rural and remote care needs to be excellent and not depend on luck. Even if it hasn't happened in 20 years, we still need to be prepared for it.

Rural and remote people deserve excellent access to health care, you'd be surprised how hard that is for some people to believe.

I also believe that affordable and accessible health care is a human right, as is the ability to seek safety. Again, not always a popular stance.

In the end, I'm an eternal optimist. The world can, and should, be a better place. If we all did a little bit extra, we could make the ordinary extraordinary.

What else helped you get to where you are?

Stubbornness, mentors, inspirational sisters. A belief that somebody has to work on these issues so it might as well be me.

Has planning or goal setting been part of your process?

I tend to have a few distant goals and then get excited by things that pop up.

What main message(s) or advice would you give others?

Treat others the way you would want to be treated in a given situation.

Growing up, to what extent did you feel different from your peers? (5 is felt on the outside, 1 easy fitted in).

A little bit different Score of 2 .

I always said that I was "born 40". Now that I am 42, I think I might have been born 50!

If the police listed you as a person of interest what would it be for?

The person who stole fun when eating in other countries. My sister says traveling with me is like travelling with the Centres for Disease Control...but she's never gotten sick on vacation with me!

What is the current project you are working on?

During the pandemic, I've chosen to stay in one rural Canadian town and work rather than travel to different ones. Staying in one place and working towards incremental change can be very challenging!

CHAPTER 11

HOLDEN SHEPPARD
(Award Winning Author)

Holden Sheppard
Credit: Jessica Gately

PROFILE

Holden Sheppard is an award-winning author born and bred in Geraldton, Western Australia.

His debut novel *Invisible Boys* (Fremantle Press) was published in 2019 to both critical and commercial success. *Invisible Boys* has won multiple accolades including the 2019 West Australian Premier's Prize for an Emerging Writer, the 2018 City of Fremantle Hungerford Award and the 2019 Kathleen Mitchell Award.

In 2020, *Invisible Boys* was shortlisted for both the Victorian Premier's Literary Awards and was named as a Notable Book by the Children's Book Council of Australia. The novel has been optioned for film and television by AACTA award-winning director Nick Verso (*Nowhere Boys, Itch, Boys in the Trees*) and producer Tania Chambers OAM (*Kill Me Three Times, A Few Less Men*).

Holden's novella *Poster Boy* was a winner of the nationwide Novella Project competition in 2018. His writing has been published in *Griffith Review, Westerly, Page Seventeen, Indigo Journal* and the *Bright Lights, No City* anthology (Margaret River Press, 2019). He has also written articles for *10 Daily*, the *Huffington Post*, the *ABC, DNA Magazine* and *Faster Louder (*now *Music Junkee*).

After graduating with Honours from Edith Cowan University's Writing program, Holden won a prestigious grant from the Australia Council for the Arts in 2015. He currently serves as Deputy Chair of WritingWA, and as an ambassador for Lifeline WA.

A lifelong misfit, Holden is a punk, a gym junkie, a player of both Aussie Rules football and Pokemon, and a bogan who learned to speak French. He lives in Perth with his husband.

Instagram: @holdensheppard   Facebook: @holdensheppardauthor   Twitter: @V8Sheppard

www.holdensheppard.com

INTERVIEW

What do you consider to be your greatest one or two achievements? (apart from family).

I know you want us to rule out family, but one of the things I am proudest of is my marriage to my husband, fellow author Raphael Farmer. It takes love, and gentleness, and healing, and empathy, and so much communication to make a marriage not just work but flourish, and I'm proud of both of us for always showing up to help each other heal and grow. But I imagine lots of people would answer with family stuff so, okay, onwards to external achievements.

My biggest career achievement to date is writing *Invisible Boys*, getting it published, and all the sales and accolades and awards. I am genuinely proud of this. It represented so many years of hard work and perseverance for me. Beyond that, the messages I get from readers who deeply related to this book are overwhelming and mean a lot to me.

I want to mention two personal achievements here I don't really talk about in media interviews, but I am proud of them because they both required courage.

The first one is getting sober.

I had a drinking problem for several years in my twenties. In my early twenties, I found myself overwhelmed by my thoughts and feelings: so much trauma, depression, anxiety and other disorders. Alcoholism isn't sexy: it ends up with a sad person drinking alone in a room because they can't handle feeling sad. That's where I was for a few years. I drank to numb myself, and it eventually spiralled out of control. I am proud of myself for getting sober and getting myself into regular therapy.

It's been five years and I'm still seeing my therapist to keep me on track. After four years sober, I gradually re-introduced small amounts of drinking back into my life, but it's carefully managed now – I only drink if it's for fun or to celebrate something with other people, as opposed to getting wasted at lunchtime just to survive the day. Getting sober and seeking help for my mental health issues changed my life.

The second personal achievement I am proud of is joining a footy team for the first time at the tender age of thirty.

As a kid I was shy and geeky, as well as generally uncoordinated, so I copped a lot of flak at school and especially in Phys Ed class. I shied away from any team sports because I was too scared I would be bad at them and did not want to invite more mockery than I already copped. I really would've loved to play AFL as a kid, but that fear was just too great.

After high school, I played a couple of seasons of seven-a-side soccer with mates, but this was with people I already knew, and not the sport I was passionate about. And once I came out as gay, I abandoned all sports: I felt there was no way I could ever fit in comfortably in a team of straight guys and so I ruled out sports.

But in early 2019, I saw a post on Facebook for an AFL team called the Perth Hornets which was Perth's first gay men's footy team. They were running a "have-a-go day" and were inviting new members down. I was so keen and excited to join, but also terrified. I can't tell you how much courage it took to rock up at that first training session – I was so scared of not fitting in, of being an absolutely useless footy player in front of guys younger than me – but I pushed myself and I did it.

Not only did I find I love playing footy, but I discovered that, while I'll never be a star footy player, I'm also not entirely incompetent and can hold my own in a team like that.

When you are celebrated for being academic and booksmart only, it can be really difficult to take a chance on something you aren't the best at, but I'm so glad I joined the Hornets – it's made a huge difference to my confidence and my life.

How do you think the life you're living is different from others?

I think what's different about working as an author is that, unlike the many years where I worked in a day job, I now wake up each day and do the thing I am most passionate about: writing.

I feel like I am following my dream every day and that, in itself, is fulfilling, regardless of external validation or success or other stimuli. Since I was a young boy, this was my dream, and I love nothing more than imagining stories and writing them down – the creative act itself is so fun and enriching for me. I feel very grateful to be able to live this life.

In some ways, being an author is similar to being any other self-employed business owner. There are plenty of mundane moments, and moments of overwork and overwhelm where work time spills into personal time. I have admin days where I am swamped with emails and phone calls, booking events and invoicing people, while managing multiple competing deadlines. I suppose the difference is that the non-admin days are pretty awesome. I get to spend time just creating and telling stories, diving into my own feelings and lived experiences to bring some version of truth to the page.

Doing public appearances, events and media is also a fun, heady part of the process (the 'fame' aspect of the job) which is perhaps interesting compared to jobs that don't have this component.

I can be an extrovert and an unabashed showpony at times, so my ego enjoys the attention and having the opportunity to share my voice and perspective with audiences.

It's also really fun to have a big part of my job be to entertain people. Whether they are reading my novels, short fiction, articles or blog posts, or just attending a talk or event of mine. I show up to give them a good time and hopefully make their investment in me worth their while.

I want people to walk away from an experience with me feeling like they have felt something, thought something, been enriched and engaged in some way ... and hopefully they had a laugh somewhere in there, too!

How did you come to live this type of life?

I've loved stories, and reading, since I was little; I started reading at three and have never lost that fascination for what a story can give to a reader.

When I was a kid, we used to go on holidays from my hometown Geraldton (a regional WA town) to Perth, four hours away. The highlight of those trips for me was getting to go to the Morley Galleria, where they had a Dymocks bookshop that totally blew my mind: it felt like we were in a big city bookshop. My parents would let me buy books each time we went to Perth. By age seven I was reading Enid Blyton's Faraway Tree and Malory Towers stories, Emily Rodda's Teen Power Inc series, and some awesome books called Usborne Puzzle Adventures, where you had to solve a puzzle or riddle or find a clue before you could turn the page.

I was so taken with books: the way you could totally escape into them and live another life far beyond who you were in the real world.

This young boy from Geraldton could imagine being in an enchanted wood in England, or a cool, sarcastic teen from Raven Hill, or an adventurous kid discovering the mysteries of a place called Demon's Cove. I never felt more alive, or enraptured, than when I was reading.

My family was driving back from one of those Perth visits in 1996 when I had the lightning bolt moment that changed my life.

I remember thinking about Enid Blyton's boarding school stories (how they were always about girls in Britain in the 1940s) and I thought how cool it would be to have a boarding school story about a boy from Australia – like me!

Of course, those books romanticised the boarding school experience, but there was a certain air of camaraderie among the characters that interested me about those books then, and still does, now: camaraderie with mates is something I live for.

Looking up at the full moon that night in the car, I realised that if I wanted a boarding school story about an Aussie boy, I could actually write it myself. It was more than that practical-level realisation, though. In that moment, I felt genuinely that writing stories was going to be my destiny, that it was what I was put on the planet to do. It was a powerful moment, and I was quite overcome with this surge of excitement within me. I couldn't wait to get started.

The next day, after school, my mum went shopping at the local supermarket and I asked for an exercise book and a four-coloured pen. This was a grown-up thing for me to do because I was in year three and we didn't get our pen licence until year five. I felt very enterprising and mature-beyond-my-years and a bit rebellious, kind of like I didn't need school to tell me what I could and couldn't do anymore.

I started writing a book called *First Form at Clifton Towers*, about a twelve-year-old boy named Jake, who went to a co-ed boarding school on a cliff. I sometimes minimise that story by joking about how the main conflict was students nearly falling off the cliff and getting saved at the last minute. The truth is when I look back at that story (I still have it), I see a tale of a boy who was lonely, who faced bullying and who was desperate to have a circle of real, true friends. I wrote fifty-six pages in that exercise book before moving on to a different story.

I was a boy with a kinetic and easily excitable mind. I had twenty or thirty books I wanted to write then, and I started lots of them but never finished any until I completed my first full "book" – maybe 10,000 words – at the age of eleven.

Sometimes I think telling this part of my story seems trite, and I wonder if people roll their eyes at it. I share it because, for me, writing was never a childhood hobby: it was always a calling and always something I took seriously, as my career. I have been a serious writer since the age of seven. I have had the same fuel and fire and ambition to achieve publication, and a career as a novelist, since this age: it's the thing I have always wanted to do.

I followed this passion through high school, studied creative writing at university and went back later for an Honours degree. I often had this vision of one day "arriving" as an author. Not a quiet moment of finally finishing a manuscript, or of signing a publishing contract: I could see a crowd cheering, and me on the stage. It was a vision of triumph. I have not often talked about this, because if I didn't make it, it would have sounded like a crazy guy with a sad dream that never came true, and now that I have been published, I feel people will think I just made it up. But I've had that vision most of my life.

When I entered the manuscript of *Invisible Boys* into the City of Fremantle Hungerford Award in 2018, I saw it in a dream again.

It was a bizarre dream where I was walking on an ice-skating rink in white socks, and then my oldest mate from primary school appeared and told me I would win the award. I was too scared to believe this dream, and I wasn't even shortlisted at the time, so I never told anyone about it.

But both the vision and dream came true on the 15th November 2018, when I won the Hungerford Award at the Fremantle Arts Centre in front of a crowd of 400 people, including family, friends and writer acquaintances who were cheering me on. I cried on stage.

It was a culmination of 22 years of hard work. I had won not just a cash prize but the publishing contract for my first ever book. I had laid hands on my holy grail, but far from being an ending, that moment was really the beginning of a much longer adventure as an author and a new way of living my life.

What, if anything, do you feel you've missed out on by living this type of life?

One of my favourite poems is *The Road Not Taken* by Robert Frost, and like Frost's narrator, I've often wondered what my life would have looked like if I had made different decisions.

My sense is that I sacrificed a whole lot of financial stability by pursuing my dream of becoming an author. At various times in my twenties, I worked full-time as a banker and later in a professional role in a university. During those times I thought I was doing what an adult was supposed to do: get a real, serious job, provide a steady income, work towards buying or building his first home.

But every time I worked full-time, I never had any time to write creatively, and this left me feeling depressed and like a total failure. I eventually gave up full time work in 2016 with no intention to ever return to it, and I never have since.

Instead, I worked part-time or casual jobs to make ends meet while making my writing career my main focus. It has meant constant stress about cash flow, little ability to buy anything cool or indulgent, and no life stability, but all of those losses are so worth it for the gaining of time to write and make being an author the core focus of my working life.

I think being an author also means I've also traded out a certain level of peace and contentedness. I don't think these things are irredeemably lost, but I do think I have at least temporarily sacrificed them. My beloved uncle recently passed away, and in doing his eulogy, which was prepared by his children, I realised how happy and contented he was with his life, and how he enjoyed his early mornings sitting on the balcony of the house he'd built, drinking a coffee and staring out at the ocean, how he lived to spend time with his family, watch the footy, and go fishing with his brother. This is a gentleness and a contentedness I would like to aspire to, but I don't have it yet.

My life as an author currently means constant hustle, and constantly aspiring for more, because it isn't until I have more books out that, I will be able to make a solid living from this career. I do look forward to the day when my income is more stable, and I can spend some time pulling back a little: hustling less, and just enjoying moments of peace and quiet, alone or with my husband or family. I think those moments are what make life special, moreso than the achievements I am lauded for.

What was your biggest challenge in achieving your goals or getting to where you are now?

It was a big challenge trying to break into the literary world as a country boy from a working-class background. My family didn't come from money, and we were living in Geraldton totally isolated from any kind of literary scene. We weren't connected with anyone influential or in the industry. I had to try to break into this world on my own, and it was very tough and disorientating.

I struggled for a long time to find out where a bogan author fits in this, at-times, very refined and snobby industry. I had to do a shit-load of networking and build up my own networks from the ground up. That was probably the hardest thing: cracking into the scene when it's not a world I'd even known about.

On a personal level, believing in myself and my writing has been a real challenge at times. I always thought I would eventually make it, but it didn't mean the journey wasn't often confused and murky and sometimes felt too hard.

Along the way did you ever think about giving up?

I never thought about giving up on writing. Not once.

I had lots of struggles, lots of hard times, a year or two where I worked full time and didn't have time to write, but they were always temporary. I always believe I would one day make it. At my core, I thought that as long as I believe it will one day happen, and I work hard to make it happen, it will happen.

Giving up was never an option. I would keep working for my dream until I died. And if I died without it coming true, okay, that sucks, but so what? I would have lived a life in pursuit of my biggest dreams. What a fulfilling way to live. I would never regret that.

What have you learnt from any difficulties or failures along the way?

Only that all success begins with failure.

When I first started really making a go of my writing, everything failed. My short stories all got rejected, grant applications were refused, even my first manuscript (a fantasy novel) was rejected by every agent who saw it.

All of those rejections hurt, but the manuscript rejection was a massive wound. That manuscript was not good enough and I had to start all over again from scratch. That heartbreak was severe. But I was determined to make it work. So, I did what was needed. I let that manuscript be a failure. I threw it in the bottom drawer.

I sat down and started working on a brand new novel from scratch, which ended up being *Invisible Boys*. It wasn't easy, but it worked. It taught me resilience and perseverance.

What kept/keeps you going? What is driving you? Is there an underlying motive?

Is it too simplistic to say "I dunno"? I've often been asked why I write and I don't have an intelligent answer for it.

It's just something I need to do, and if I don't do it I get sick – not physically necessarily but emotionally. My soul gets sick if I don't express myself creatively for too long. I crave being expressed as honestly as possible. I think it helps me process my own emotions and get a sense of who I am. This is probably what drives me. I suppose I am mostly driven by that need to be seen, and for catharsis.

In terms of motive, I would write regardless. But I get a kick out of the idea that my writing can help others.

I have had many, many messages from readers of *Invisible Boys* who were brought to tears by the book. So many have said that my book put into words what they went through as teenagers. Many people, especially gay men, have told me this book helped them to process the trauma they went through in their younger years. It helps some people to heal. I am grateful for that outcome, and motivated to hopefully keep showing up as authentically as I can in my art to potentially help others process their own feelings.

What else helped you get to where you are? E.g. Are there any personal qualities that have helped you?

Blind ambition. Absolute doggedness.

Hard work and the willingness to grind and hustle.

Vulnerability – it is essential to make good art.

Self-care – it is essential to prioritise this in order to survive being a vulnerable artist.

And a massive ego: I think it's essential, that unwavering self-belief, to make something of yourself, because the world will constantly try to bring you back down to reality and put you back in your place. You have to have the ego to match up and hold your ambitions on its shoulders.

Other people have also helped me a lot. My husband is a huge source of strength and support: he is my first reader and my champion. Same for my family members, mates, writer buddies, industry people, agents. Having people cheering you on and supporting you makes a big difference.

And it only happens if you're putting that energy out to others, too, so that's what I do: support others with big dreams and receive support in return.

What's your attitude to planning and goal setting? Do you always have to be working toward a goal or do you take life as it comes?

Goal-setting is like crack to me.

I set new goals every New Year's Eve or New Year's Day and work hard to achieve them. It keeps me focused and on track and ensures I spend my time prioritising the projects and activities that actually matter to me. My annual goals will comprise career stuff e.g. writing goals, plus personal stuff (gym workouts, footy, learning guitar) and so on.

I am realistic. I know I usually don't achieve all my goals for the year. Most years it's maybe fifty percent. I don't beat myself up if I didn't achieve a goal in a given year. I reassess at the end of that year. If I still want it, it goes back on the list. I'll get there eventually.

I can be easy-going in some settings. For example, on holidays or having drinks with mates, but when it comes to life ambitions, I'm pretty intense. It's the only way I can get anything done.

What main message(s) or advice would you give others thinking about living a life outside the norm?

Do it.

If you succeed, it will be amazing.

If you fail, you will have spent your entire life pursuing something you love.

Either way, you will live a life you won't regret and it will be a more fulfilling life than anything else you would have otherwise done.

Also, fuck the haters. Striving for a life outside the norm almost inevitably leads to Tall Poppy Syndrome. People will seek to cut you back down to size. This will include family members and friends who don't like the idea of losing their closeness to you or are jealous of you. It sucks but it's part of the process. If people are not supportive, and are dragging you down rather than championing you, don't give them your time. Spend time around people who love you unconditionally and lift you up the way you lift them up.

Growing up to what extent, if at all, did you feel different from your peers?

Very different.

I've always had bigger ambitions than most of my peers, which personally didn't faze me, but the reaction I got from them was one of misunderstanding, or jealousy, or that I thought I was too big for my boots. I always felt a bit odd, a highly-sensitive artist amid a sea of people who seemed less affected by feelings.

To what extent did you feel you fitted into society when you were growing ? (5 is felt on the outside, 1 easy fitted in).

Didn't feel I fitted in 5.

I grew up in a country town – boys were meant to be rough and tough, not academic or creative or sensitive. Outwardly, I was shy and reserved and this made me not cool at school. It wasn't until I left high school that I found a lot more confidence and realised that you can be rough and tough but also sensitive. I'm all about wholeness now. But growing up, I was firmly an outsider.

If the Police listed you as a person of interest what would it be for, and why?

Public indecency, no question. I have a tendency to take off my shirt for selfies a lot, and I may have a history of moonings and nudie runs.

What is the current project you're working on that you'd like promoted?

I've had the film and TV rights for *Invisible Boys* optioned, so it's being made into a TV series which is hell exciting. I'll be involved in the writers' room so I'm looking forward to being a part of that creative process of translating the book to the screen.

CHAPTER 12

IAN USHER (Freedom Lifestyle Speaker, Author)

Ian Usher
Credit: Ian Usher

HOW I MET IAN USHER

I first heard about Ian Usher around 2008 when I read an article about a local man selling his life on eBay, perhaps you remember that too. Ian's "life" for sale consisted of a nice suburban house, furniture, some big boy toys (e.g. a jet ski, motorbike), an introduction to his old boss and friends, but not his wife Laura as she'd decided to pull up stumps. Laura's departure, and subsequently finding himself standing on a bridge one night contemplating life, was the catalyst for change.

At the time my life was also at a crossroad having lost my partner three years earlier. I was just starting to emerge from the grief fog when I read the article about Ian. It was the third time in my life that my mindset had shifted towards saying "yes" to whatever possibilities came my way. My overwhelming feeling was one of being lost in a foreign world. Consequently, I began searching for something, anything, that would take my life outside the norm. Ian appeared as somewhat of a kindred spirit, albeit a lot braver than I.

The article must have mentioned a website and contact details as somehow one day I found myself sitting across the table from Ian in a café at Innaloo Shopping Centre. The details of how that came about are a little hazy now.

Hours of chat later I'd come to realise that this stranger wasn't an axe-murderer, which is handy for any first meeting. Not only that he was open, easy to talk to, held good values and was just trying to make his way through life as best he could. The meet-up ended with me taking a quick ride around the neighbourhood on the back of his motorbike, something I hadn't done for years. The fact that I was prepared to get on the back of a strangers (possible axe-murders) motorbike speaks volumes about my mindset at the time.

As we first took off, my author brain wrote the first chapter of a novel about a naïve woman being kidnapped and killed. But that soon passed as I realised he was sticking to the block I'd mapped out. After swapping numbers, and an invitation to join him on any part of his journey, we went our separate ways.

Over the years, as my life settle back into a gentler ride, I kept an eye on Ian's progress and stayed in touch sporadically online. He has led a fascinating life as you will see.

PROFILE

Usher grew up in England and following school he lived on a kibbutz in Israel then travelled through Europe. In 1985 he gained a teaching degree in Outdoor Education at Liverpool Polytechnic. He worked with British Rail as a Youth Leadership and Teamwork Counsellor before opening Scarborough Jet Skiing on England's north east coast.

In 2001 he moved to Australia where he worked in sales, marketing and management. It was this job that he included in his eBay Life For Sale in 2008.

The sale gained worldwide attention, particularly when the bids quickly spiralled over a million dollars. Sadly, those bids turned out to be bogus. The final value of his life was $399,300. The question was what to do next?

A US agent posed this very question to Ian pointing out that whatever he did next could set himself up for life. No pressure!

This prompted Ian to write a list of all the things he wanted to do. That list turned into the website called *100 Goals In 100 Weeks,* and the goal setting period of his life. Amongst the goals were the usual sights to see, but also some more unusual goals including meet Richard Branson. Before you think this all sounds very hedonistic, the list also included raising funds for Colon Cancer, something close to Ian's family.

The list of goals were getting ticked off, not just by Ian but anyone who wanted to join him along the way. And so, a small community of like-minded people began to form.

After two years the adventure ended on 4 July 2010 on top of the Statue of Liberty. In an ending, beloved by Hollywood, but grounded in truth in Ian's case, the adventure also ended in love, when Usher found his partner Vanessa.

A book followed, *A Life Sold*, and the movie rights were purchased by Walt Disney Pictures who commissioned a project called *Life for Sale.*

With his soulmate by his side what did Ian do next? Did they ride off together into a standard 4 by 2 home and work in adjoining cubicles? No.

Why not live on your own private Caribbean island?

With a desire to live off-grid, in 2011 Ian researched and bought a remote Panamanian island in the Caribbean, a mere speck on the map. Usher's Island was born. There they cleared the land and built an off-grid home, beginning with a jetty for the barge that transported everything to the island. Once again, Usher allowed anyone to be part of the journey by following his progress online or popping over to the island to help out. Three years later the mission was accomplished, and various television crews came a calling.

A second book followed in 2013, with the title *Paradise Delayed,* hinting at some of the problems experienced along the way.

At about this time Usher was called on to present inspirational talks for companies in the USA and Europe, along with a TEDxVienna talk to 900 people.

You'd think that would be it but no.

In 2014 Usher began contemplating life again wondering ...

"Is this it. I thought it would be better than this. This isn't the life I dreamt of", said Usher.

Thoughts of living a nomadic life surfaced. A life with no home and few possessions. Unbelievably after all that hard work he sold the Caribbean island. Actually, it took a couple of years to sell the island. But ultimately he and his partner were debt-free and with a small bank balance. What to do?

First up they spent six months in an RV (Recreational Vehicle) travelling around the south west of the USA. Then for the next six years they set about designing a "Freedom Lifestyle".

In 2015 they spent a year in China teaching English.

Working for themselves and with no fixed address, they began travelling the world taking advantage of opportunities. As a result, they have been house sitting around 11 countries in six years, while visiting 12 other countries between assignments. They also started an online business to create a passive income. This includes selling website services, teaching English and housesitting courses. Along the way they have published a free House Sitting magazine and run a similarly themed conference.

www.IanUsher.com and HouseSittingMagazine.com

INTERVIEW

What do you consider to be your greatest one or two achievements? (apart from family).

I think that turning my life around from a low point of separation in 2006, and the subsequent divorce in 2008, to build a life filled with travel, adventure and freedom, was the most defining choice of my life.

I could so easily have chosen to wallow in self-pity, and gone back to life as it was before, or rather a shadow of that former life, with the most important part of it gone forever.

But the choice I made was a complete new start, with an unknown path ahead, offering challenges and experiences that I could have never imagined before taking the bold step out of my comfort zone.

That choice led on to other significant achievements. The 100 weeks of the 100 goals adventure is the biggest, most sustained effort I have ever put into any single project, and I'm very proud of what I achieved.

I am also proud of the inspiration all of my choices along the way gave to other people.

Building the off-grid property on the little island in Panama was also an achievement of which I am very proud ... in fact living that amazing boat-based lifestyle, learning all I needed to learn to get by in a completely different environment, was fun and challenging.

What was your biggest challenge in achieving your goals or getting to where you are now?

There have been many challenges along the way, each different adventure offering its own hurdles to overcome.

On a personal basis, one of my biggest challenges is seeing things through to the end. I tend to get things about 80 to 90% complete, then tend to find my attention drifting to the next big adventure. I think that is why I am proud of the big things I did see through to final completion.

It is something I am still working on.

Along the way did you ever think about giving up?

Many times.

When I look back at the 100 goals adventure, there were many occasions when I questioned why I was doing what I was doing. There were financial challenges, time constraints, loneliness, and "what's the point of this?" moments. It often seemed very appealing to just stop, settle and make things easier on myself.

What have you learnt from any difficulties or failures along the way?

It might sound like a "motivational quote" stock answer, but it really is true that if we don't risk failure, we can't achieve challenging goals. All we can do is give it our best shot, look upon any failures as learning opportunities, and get back up and try a different approach to the problem.

Another thing I discovered... some of our best memories and funniest stories come from the difficult times we face. I always laugh about a toothbrush moment in a cheap little backstreet hotel in Kathmandu in Nepal. It seemed like the lowest point of my journey at the time, but it puts a huge smile on my face whenever I think about it. (see www.ianusher.com 100 goals in 100 weeks, high-peaks-and-low-troughs and last-day-in Kathmandu-I-hope).

What kept/keeps you going? Is there an underlying motive?

I really just want to live the best, most interesting life I can. I believe we only get one go at this, and I just want to experience as much variety as life can offer. I don't want to reach the end of the journey with too many regrets about the things I didn't do.

I believe life is about experience. In order to fit as much new experience into the short time we all have, it is important to keep moving forward. Let's not forget, that we are all going to die one day.

We're not rich, we're not retired, and we don't have a huge fund of savings behind us. We're a pretty normal couple who have made some decisions that have taken us way outside the norm. We haven't done anything that most others couldn't decide to do, if they wished to follow in our footsteps.

What else helped you get to where you are?

I think one of the best assets you can develop is a curiosity about everything around you. This makes learning new skills a fun challenge, meeting new people an interesting experience, and travelling to new places the one of the most stimulating aspects of life's possibilities. I'm always interested in learning new things.

What, if anything, do you feel you've missed out on by living this type of life?

By living a lifestyle with no real home base for extended periods of time means you miss out on the comforts and pleasures of having friends and family close by.

But I think all major life choices involve some sort of trade-off, and what you gain in one area, you lose something in another. Taking a new job in a new company may mean a better salary, but perhaps you'll have to move away from your current social circle. Travelling the world means you lose touch with many people over the years, but you meet many new friends too.

You have to make your own assessment of the win/lose balance and change your actions if your choices aren't giving you the results you desire.

What's your attitude to planning and goal setting?

I'm actually taking life much more as it comes, and now just set shorter term goals in much smaller numbers than previously.

The current pandemic, and how Europe seems to be handling (or mis-handling?) it, means that any travel goals have had to be put on hold, as have many other plans for the future, until we see how this all pans out.

Being flexible. Prepared to react to changing circumstances, seems more important at the moment than any longer term goals.

What main message(s) would you give others thinking about living a life outside the norm?

If it appeals, then do it.

Assess what is the worst that could happen, then take steps to ensure that worst possible outcome doesn't happen. Even if things go badly, it won't be as emotionally painful or damaging as the regrets you'll carry forever about not following your dreams.

Growing up, to what extent did you feel different from your peers?

I've always got on well with a wide range of people and have never felt like an outsider.

But on the other hand I was never a great team player in school sports. Nor have I ever been a particularly good employee. I tend to like to do things my own way, so can't claim box number 1 as "easily fitted in".

If the Police listed you as a person of interest what would it be for?

I think I would probably feature on the "wanted" list because of endless minor infractions of petty rules.

Some laws just don't seem to make any sense, and I can't bear bureaucratic red tape. Most of the times I have had any sort of run-in with authority figures have been at border crossings, where they want to see proof of an onward flight or tell me I can't travel without paying some ridiculous money-grabbing fee for a visa.

What is the current project you're working on?

Living a *Freedom Lifestyle* and helping others do the same. For more information go to www.ianusher.com/freedom-lifestyle.

I have put any "freedom" writings on hold at the moment, because we don't currently have much at all. We (Vanessa and I) are still trying to live a varied and interesting lifestyle, and are currently in France, but going anywhere else, even back to the UK right now, is getting harder and harder.

We're still house sitting as much as we can here in France and enjoying in-between sits small adventures in our little campervan.

CHAPTER 13

25 LESSONS LEARNT

I hope you enjoyed reading about these fascinating people as much as I did interviewing them. Thanks to their generosity and openness we've identified the following 25 lessons:

Lesson 1: No Prerequisite To An Interesting Life

While some of the interviewees had gone on to gain higher education, not everyone had. A formal education is not a prerequisite to living an interesting life and making a positive impact on the world.

Lesson 2: A Profession Is Not For Life

Some of those who had gone to university (or entered a professional field) had taken a step sideways and opened up a whole new world of interest. Just because you're trained in one profession doesn't mean you have to be closed off to other opportunities that might arise. The skills learnt in one profession can often be transferred to another.

Lesson 3 Anyone Can Feel Like An Outsider

The definition of an Outsider is ...

> *Someone who is not accepted as a member of a particular group, organisation or society and who feels different from those people who are accepted as members.*

No doubt the definition will conjure up some images in your mind. Perhaps someone living outside the law, someone from a different background or with a disability to name just a few of the stereotypical imagery.

As stated earlier, it was fascinating to hear several of the initial interviewees say they felt like outsiders, as they did not fit the stereotypical images. I started to wonder if there was another subsegment, a group of "Hidden Outsiders" perhaps.

To explore further I added another question to the questionnaire - a rating scale where people self-reported their perception of "fitting in", either at school or life in general.

I also changed my interviewee criteria slightly. After much deliberation I decided to consciously ignore people who fitted the stereotypes. I was interested in exploring the idea of "Hidden Outsiders." I thought this might also be of interest to the high school students.

As shown in the comments, anyone can feel like an outsider, regardless of whether they fit the stereotypes or not. As usual stereotypes can be misleading. Once again, we are reminded not to judge a book by its cover.

Lesson 4 Not Fitting In Can Be Motivating

The comments suggested that not fitting in can be a motivating factor. For some it made them look at life differently. This in turn can result in innovations that benefit everyone.

Lesson 5 Know yourself

There was a lot of talk amongst interviewees about trusting your gut, backing yourself, knowing your strengths and your shortcomings, but not letting them hold you back. Chris Morgan reminded us that no one is going to do it for you, "you have to do it for yourself". Megan Simpson Huberman talked about backing yourself for a year, then reassessing the outcomes. She added that her life experiences as a woman of her age were her "superpowers."

Lesson 6 Practice and work hard

Interviewees were focused on working hard and being aware that nothing is given to you. They spoke about practice and doing what you're trying to achieve again and again and again. About keeping on with the grind, the hustle, about dedication and passion. Dr Olga Ward said it's about "doing a good job, not an adequate job" and Chris Morgan added it's "knowing that you get out what you put in."

Lesson 7 Plan, but be flexible

In terms of planning the interviewees were divided. Some were of the belief that you had to plan ahead if you wanted to achieve anything, as life has a habit of getting in the way. We were reminded that life is about preparation meeting opportunity and staying ahead of the changes.

For others it depended on which aspect of their work they were focusing on. Some areas were well planned, others were left to their creative flow.

Overall, most added the need to be flexible in your plans. Tineke Van der Eecken presented an interesting angle of not overthinking where you are headed because "life is more interesting if you let things emerge." Ian Usher pointed out that being flexible was even more important "at the moment", and that you can always "change your actions if your choices aren't giving you the results you desire."

Lesson 8 Self doubt

Often we see people achieving great things, but we don't see the many times they thought about giving up. There will definitely be times when you think about giving up. There will be doubts. It's a matter of how you react to them.

Ian Usher suggested thinking "what is the worst thing that can happen, then take steps to ensure that doesn't happen". He added that "even if things do go badly it won't be as emotionally painful as the regrets of never having done it in the first place".

Lesson 9 Ignore the doubters

There was considerable discussion about ignoring "the Doubters". About not being put off by family "advice", or "the Knockers". Interviewees suggested putting these comments aside and focusing on what you want to do. To not get hung up about others expectations. As Holden Sheppard said "striving for a life outside the norm almost inevitably leads to Tall Poppy Syndrome."

Lesson 10 Ignore the first "no"

Several interviewees described themselves as having an element of stubbornness. This included the ability to ignore the first time they heard the word "no". Instead of hearing "no" as an end point it can simply mean going back to the drawing board and trying again.

Lesson 11 Develop good communication skills

Several interviewees also mentioned speaking up, asking questions and questioning peers or mentors. Dr Olga Ward reminded us that "the squeaky wheels get oiled" and Dr Sarah Giles said "sometimes you can catch more flies with honey." Megan Simpson Huberman provided another perspective saying "interpersonal skills are crucial". Adding that "you need to have a vision but to be able to share your vision with others and be open to their ideas." She also believed that "talent makes up 40% and collaboration is 60%."

Lesson 12 Network

Interviewees spoke about network in the industry you aim to be a part of. For collaborations, seek to work with people who are aligned with your values and have skills that complement yours. Dr Olga Ward suggested joining committees to make changes from within.

When networking just make sure you listen to the right people. If you're not sure about the advice you're receiving take a moment to think about who it's coming from. Do they have any vested interests in your success ... or failure?

Lesson 13 Support others

They reminded us that while networking for your own needs is important, it is equally important to support others in their quest.

Lesson 14 Motivation, why do it?

In terms of motivation some interviewees talked about wanting to be "in control" of their own destiny. Others reminded us that external motivations such as creating things "to get likes" is not sustainable. Jason Chatfield suggested it was more important to "create for yourself" and that people who liked your work would find you.

Tineke Van der Eecken said "it's not money but experiences that would make you grow." Meanwhile Ian Usher said he was just trying to "live the best most interesting life I can".

Lesson 15 Disability/Poor Health As A Catalyst

While compiling the interviews it was interesting to hear several of the interviewees mention an illness or disability. What was particularly interesting was how this was often mentioned as a throw away, secondary thought. While this ill health was part of their life, no doubt a big part, it certainly didn't stop their quest to live an interesting life. In some cases it was the catalyst to seek their purpose.

Lesson 16 A World view motivation

There was some discussions about looking beyond the self and acting in ways to help the world. For example Tineke Van der Eecken felt the world "is a better place than the media portray", and that we are "collectively responsible to make this world a better place". Dr Sarah Giles added "the world can and should be a better place, if we all did a little bit extra we could make the ordinary, extraordinary". She added that "somebody has to work on these issues it might as well be me."

Lesson 17 Embrace Difficulties

Several interviewees talked about seeing difficulties as learning opportunities. The focus was on getting back up and trying a different approach. Holden Sheppard said "all success begins with failure". Tim Ferguson reminded us that "because everything is always changing you always have the chance and the time to change tracks" and when one door closes "kick in another one". Ian Usher added "if we don't risk failure, we can't achieve challenging goals."

Lesson 18 Don't throw the baby out with the bathwater

Chris Morgan gave us a lesson from drag racing to not rush to change everything. That while it might take more time, "by changing just one thing then checking to see the impact", we will learn which elements of our plans work and which don't.

Lesson 19 Keep moving forwards

Interviewees talked about the importance of not plateauing, of continually moving forward, being curious, having an enquiring mind, learning and taking on new opportunities as they arose. Ian Usher said "the best assets you can develop is a curiosity about everything around you." He also felt it's important to keep moving forward, "let's not forget we're all going to die someday".

Lesson 20 Distractions

While being open to new opportunities is important, we were also reminded not to get distracted. To stay the course on the projects that are important to us.

Lesson 21 Selfcare

A few of the interviewees reminded us that life is a balancing act and selfcare is essential to succeed. That it is important to treat your future self well.

Lesson 22 Vulnerability is okay

While talking about selfcare, some interviewees stressed that vulnerability is okay. In fact it is essential in creative fields. Trying to hide your vulnerability can result in ill health.

Lesson 23 They are not special

As seen through the comments, none of the interviewees considered themselves unique or blessed with special powers. They have taught us that anyone can live an interesting life outside the norm. As Ian Usher said "we haven't done anything that most others couldn't decide to do if they wish to follow in our footsteps."

Lesson 24 Have a go

Most of all the interviewees urged people to have a red hot go, have a crack or just do it. As pointed out by Holden Sheppard "if you succeed it will be amazing if you fail you have spent your entire life pursuing something you love".

Lesson 25 Think Big And Keep Positive

The profiles and interviews have inspired me to think bigger and keep positive. As Tim Ferguson said "if your boat sinks in the ocean, people who stay positive survive."

If you know someone who should be featured please let me know.

Good luck in your adventures and make sure you have fun along the way to becoming a *Person Of Interest.*

Glennys

www.glennysmarsdon.com
Facebook: Glennys Marsdon author
Insta: @glennysmarsdon

ABOUT THE AUTHOR

ABOUT THE AUTHOR

Marsdon's passion for people saw her qualify as a psychologist in the 1980s, then spend over 20 years studying consumer behaviour.

Through her independent consumer psychology consultancy, *The Customers' Voice*, she's helped numerous organisations develop marketing plans, advertising campaigns and new products. She's also delved into a wide range of social issues, from the youth drug culture to domestic violence, caring and retirement. All of this has enabled her to interact with a diverse range of people, a need that grew out of her first job with the Australian Red Cross, where she spent three years travelling around Western Australia to places like Useless Loop.

While at the Australian Red Cross she was responsible for the *Youth News* magazine, which went out to all West Australian schools.

In 2007 she published her first book, *50 Ways To Grieve Your Lover,* which was taken up by counsellors working in the Victorian Bush Fires and New Zealand Pike Mine Disaster. As a result, she was profiled in a book by American marketing guru Seth Godin, called *Tales of the Revolution: True Stories About People Making A Difference.*

Due to the success of the book she started a blog called *The Ponder Room* which attracted an international audience across 20+ countries after just six months.

In 2008 she wrote her first piece of fiction '*A Whales Tale*', which won first prize in the Stirling Adult Literary Awards.

This led to more freelance writing including a monthly column in *Swan Magazine* and the *MX5 Magazine*, regular gigs with on and off line magazines including, *Visit Perth City, Tweet Perth, The Weekly Review* (Melbourne), *Divine* (Disability) and *ABC Ramp It Up* to name a few.

In 2010 she received the Rigby Award for services to cartooning due to her work on the Michael Collins Caricature Award, a national award which was established to honour her partner. The Award ran successfully for four years, each year donating all the proceeds to the Heart Foundation.

In 2012 she was nominated for a Telstra Business Women's Award, and in 2013 her second book *Me Time 100 Strategies For Guilt Free Me Time*, landed her a People's Choice Award.

In 2020 faced with no income due to the Covid pandemic she undertook a survey of USA and Australian residents to explore what they had learnt about themselves and life in general. The book went on to sell well in the US.

She currently spreads her time between freelance research and writing jobs, plus sitting on a number of advisory Boards, conducting workshops and personal mentoring sessions. The workshop topics include - Personal Branding, Consumer Psychology, Writing Your First Book, Overcoming Grief and Gaining Guilt Free Me Time.

OTHER BOOKS BY GLENNYS MARSDON

- Covid 19: 60 Lessons Learnt About Life And Yourself (WA & USA)
- Life After Covid19: 35 Strategies To Maintain (USA & WA comments)
- 50 Ways To Grieve Your Lover: 100 Tips Gaining Back Control
- 30 Tips To Successfully Work At Home: Based on 20+yrs experience
- Me Time: 100 Strategies For Guilt Free Me Time.
- Freelance Life: An Action Plan To Help You Become A Successful Six Figure Freelancer
- Wit And Wisdom: A Collection Of Essays From The Most Isolated City
- Gluteus Maximus There She Blows: Short story (competition winner)
- A Bouquet of Love (Fiction Anthology)
- All Wrapped Up (Fiction Anthology)
- Sunk (Short Fiction - Romantic comedy)

For more information go to www.glennysmarsdon.com '

Or contact Glennys via email admin@glennysmarsdon.com